The Truth Does Set Us Free

I Was Spiritually Bankrupt and
Didn't Even Know It!

Kathleen E. Brummer

InspiringVoices®

Scriptures taken from The Jerusalem Bible © 1966 by Darton Longman & Todd Ltd and Doubleday and Company Ltd.

Inspiring Voices books may be ordered through booksellers or by contacting:

Inspiring Voices
1663 Liberty Drive
Bloomington, IN 47403
www.inspiringvoices.com
1 (866) 697-5313

ISBN: 978-1-4624-1117-7 (sc)
ISBN: 978-1-4624-1118-4 (e)

Library of Congress Control Number: 2015905281

Print information available on the last page.

Inspiring Voices rev. date: 05/15/2015

Contents

Introduction

The Truth DOES Set Us Free:
I was Spiritually Bankrupt and Didn't Even Know it!

"**Spiritual** 1. Of the spirit or the soul, often in a religious or moral aspect, as distinguished from the body. 2. Of, from, or concerned with the intellect, or what is often thought of as the better or higher part of the mind. 3. Of, or consisting of spirit, not corporal. 4. Characterized by the ascendancy of the spirit; showing much refinement of thought and feeling. 5. Of religion or the church; sacred, devotional, or ecclesiastical; not lay or temporal.

Bankruptcy [Fr. *banqueroute*; It. *banca* (bench) + *rotta* (broken) L. *rupius* pp of *rumpere*, (to break)] 1. A person legally declared unable to pay his debts; the property of a bankrupt is divided among his creditors or administered for their benefits. 2. Loosely, anyone unable to pay his debts. 3. A person who lacks a certain quality: as a mental bankrupt."

All definitions are taken from the
"Webster's New World Dictionary of the
American Language" *College Edition*

How could two such things possibly fit together? And where does *truth* fit in? One definition of truth is "*the quality of being in accordance with experience, facts or reality*". We each seem to have different ideas of what *truth* might be; after all our experiences can be perceived in many ways! All of these words speak to corner stones which have become the foundation of my learning and journey. They have led me to a freedom I couldn't have imagined for myself.

I best start from the beginning, for you to appreciate how these fit together for me, and to help you appreciate the huge awakening that I experienced at the age of 30.

Part 1

My Beginnings

Chapter 1

Growing Up

I grew up in a larger family, on a farm. We were creative, hard workers and knew that we were needed to take care of chickens, cattle, the summer garden and large yard. I was a middle child. For some reason, I was very tied in with my mother and her feelings. I did not understand why this was; I just could intuit that she had sadness buried inside. Although Mom loved people who brought humor and lightness to her days, overall she felt that life was serious, and had many fears which affected me. I took on the role of peacemaker with my siblings. We had pride in our accomplishments and abilities. But I did not know that all of this had a personal expense. As I grew, I buried my feelings. I used food to find a release from them and found consolation in carbohydrates and sugars. Baking was always available in our home; we had a 'bread drawer' and cookie jar in the pantry. We would bake goodies every Saturday morning for the week's use. I grew to hide my eating as I overate; later, I realized that this was connected with my feeling of shame about my behavior.

I have memories of being eight years old. I chose – like a good girl – to give up candy for lent (a forty day period of penance and fasting before Easter). But at age eight, I could no longer stay away from sweets and candy for an extended period. I had succeeded in this Lenten fast as a six and seven-year old, but now couldn't understand sugar's call to me and my inability to stay away from it.

By the time I was in eighth grade, I was wearing 'chubby girls' sizes. I chose fashions that I felt would hide my extra weight. I was a very sensitive person, and quite religious. It was a part of our week to go to church on Sundays, and pray together at meals, and as a family in the evening. These practices were important to us, even though our prayers were rote. God was somewhere outside of me, although I sensed God's presence in our church and in our liturgical celebrations. I wanted to be a good person and live an exemplary life.

At the end of that school year, I attempted an 'eggs and grapefruit' diet and lost about 18 pounds. And boy did I like the way that I looked and felt! This was timely for me, because I would attend a 'city' school in ninth grade, after attending country schools to this point. The thought of fitting in with 'city kids' scared me.

I was very self-conscious, but felt good wearing smaller sized clothing as I transitioned to this new school. And I felt that I had learned a new secret to help me deal with my weight struggles…dieting.

I remember thinking – during those high school years - that if there was such a thing as a 'foodaholic', it might describe me. For some reason, I noticed that I seemed to like food more than most people! I didn't understand this.

I lived in my head a lot. I constructed a fantasy life and loved to read books - to enter into their world of fun and adventure. It was a part of my way of coping.

The God of my youth had a mixture of qualities. God was 'judge' and I searched to appease 'him' by doing good deeds. God watched and knew everything about me. I *was* told, by my Mom who was forever working, that I would be held accountable for every minute that I 'wasted' in this life. No wonder why I became a human-*doing* before I could learn to be a human-*being*!

And I *did* excel at doing. Artistic and musical, interested in organizing and building things with my hands, I forever was in the *middle* of a project. I speak the truth here, for my projects didn't always find their way to completion!

Don't get me wrong; those years were not all work and no play. I knew the feeling of being needed and appreciated. I also knew the satisfaction of working with the land, of getting to know birds and flowers and discovering the personality of some of the different animals – pets and livestock we had on our farm. Though my days held ongoing chores and jobs to do, there was always a sense of wonder and delight that I felt as I learned about nature. Our Dad and Mom were great teachers.

I have a memory of dad driving the tractor home from the field, holding a branch with a possum clinging to it for dear life; he wanted his children to see this animal, which was not common in our area. Sometimes he'd get us to come out of the house to see an unusual bird. At night, he would show us the stars and their constellations.

Now Mom was a gardener. I learned a lot about flowers and vegetables from her, both how to grow them and how to preserve them for future meals. She, too, loved our farm animals. Mom always felt sorry for them when it was time to take them to market, or when a calf was old enough to be sold, leaving its' mother literally 'crying out' in sadness for several days. She always said that she knew what it felt like to 'be a mother'.

There were parts of my mother that I didn't understand. She had a very kind heart, yet I was raised with the message that immodesty was *sinful*. This may well be what she was taught. As my body began to change in my teen years, I didn't know what to do with feelings of attraction to boys. I could sense that Mom feared the thought of me dating.

I didn't go to many dances. I was not outgoing as a result of my awkwardness with boys, self-consciousness and my developing body. Being 'forward' with boys was not considered appropriate; so I dreamt of magically attracting someone into my life. There was a tug of war within myself about such things.

At 18, I went to my first wedding dance. Because I had very little experience with dancing and felt awkward, I was hesitant to venture out. But I did enter into the 'circle 2 step' dance. At one point, my Mom nudged my Dad, telling him that he should take me out on the dance floor. He did. And shortly into our dance, he said something that still tickles my heart. He said, "Get light on your feet!!" How in the heck was I supposed to do that??

Later at the dance, I met a guy my age who reached out to me; I joined him in his 'booth'. We visited for a while, before it was time to leave. When I went up to my bedroom that evening after the dance, I remember crying... "I'm *not* ugly!" Up to that point, having not 'attracted' any boys to be interested in dating me, I came to assume that I was unattractive.

About a week later, as I came home from high school, Mom walked up to the refrigerator to reach for something. On it, she had a letter that I had received in the mail. It was from the guy that I met at the dance! But her words left me not knowing what to do... "*Now* look at what you started!" As I shared earlier, I always attempted to please my Mom. I never responded to his letter. But, later in the school year, I asked this guy to go to prom with me, and he did.

Spirituality, how I lived out my beliefs, was always important to me. That summer, I made the decision to enter the convent as two of my older sisters had done. For me, it came from a desire to know God better. And, I wanted to please God and subconsciously, my mother. Because my older sisters were in the convent, I had a positive impression as I came to see their way of life. They had chosen a teaching order of sisters; which attracted me. Also I was not world – wise and felt intimidated at the thought of going off to a larger public or private college. So enter the convent I did.

Personally, my search for God there was a dry one. Yet, I delighted in our liturgies and the music connected with them. I had many opportunities to become involved in that music, and to begin studies with a major in music. Because I continued to stuff my feelings, my eating and my weight hit an all-time high during that time.

I made several life-long friends there. We started each day with Lauds, and then in the evening prayed Vespers and sometimes Compline. We also celebrated Mass daily. I was one of 24 that entered together. We pitched in with laundry, big scale for our large community and with cleaning although the majority of our days were spent attending classes to further our education. We did have fun too; I can still remember some of the crazy pranks we pulled! I've never regretted exploring that way of life, but it was not for me.

It took five years for me to realize that. Deep in my heart, I had always desired a husband and children. And living in community, with an ever – changing group of people did not fit me well. I feared what my Mom would say, but chose to move ahead into unknown territory for myself. In the end, I found relief as I experienced the blessing of many of my fellow Sisters on my decision. And, one day in the following months at home, I overheard my Mother say, "Kathy wasn't happy there." What a relief that was for me!

Going out into the wide world scared me, but I did have a degree in teaching. A Sister and a Priest friend took me under their wings and connected me with a job opportunity, which I felt fit me. They helped me connect with a party that had a vacant upstairs apartment near my new job and were even helpful in getting a bed for me to use!

As much as I desired dating, that part of my life developed slowly. Living alone was very painful; I did not know myself, nor was I at peace with myself. During my second year, I met a divorced man of another faith - which, in my mind gave him two strikes against my dating him! But I was so hungry for dating that I went out with him. In the end, he was very respectful toward me, but suddenly stopped calling. I felt crazy wondering why! For me, this opened the door for some of my first attempts to identify and communicate my feelings. I was unable to speak with him for some time; he made himself scarce. But I had friends in some of my co-workers and could share with them.

I did feel complimented as two fellow teachers asked if they might line up a blind date for me with family members! Those went fine, but no friendship was sparked.

I grew to listen to my insides even more. Living alone was painful for me, so I let it be known that I would welcome living with a room-mate. And I learned of someone who was looking for one as well. I moved in with her; her company and presence helped me greatly in my day-to-day life. She even lined up a blind date for me with her boyfriend's brother!

This gal soon announced her engagement. About the same time, I felt the inner urge to look for a new job, moving out of the city that I was in. I knew enough to listen to this urge and started to consider where I might next work and live.

My area of work was quite new in the southern part of our state. When others learned that I might be available they contacted me, asking if I might like to interview with them!! Before long, I had **eight** job prospects. Wow, did I ever feel that I was being led! I listened to my heart and chose a few to pursue in depth.

One stood out - in my mind – so I gave notice and agreed to take this new job.

This choice was truly an act of faith for me, because I wanted to meet someone to date...and chose a job in a community where the number of females greatly outnumbered the number of males! There were large hospitals and clinics in this community, so many nurses were drawn to work there. And, at this time, male nurses were quite the exception! But it was a good job for me. I couldn't know that the following years would open the door to meeting my husband – to – be, and to a great awakening.

Chapter 2

My Journey Continues

I'll never forget my feelings as I drove from the community of my first job to the new job that I had chosen to take. I knew almost no one in this new community. Many of my friends were behind me as I drove those 41 miles. And, I had almost everything that I owned in my little Dodge Colt! I called my car 'pickles' because that name fit its' color...I had purchased it about 6 months before to get myself to work from my second apartment.

I knew that I'd be happiest living with someone, so as I explored this job, I asked and learned that a music teacher in another school was looking for someone to share her apartment with. I checked out this possibility and chose to move in.

My new Pastor was like a warm father figure for me. Over that first month, it was my 'dream' to go to Europe and Rome with a friend. My sister lived in Rome and it would be a chance to visit her, plus see a new part of the world. I had paid vacation time saved up from my first job. But to do this, I would need to take the first month 'off' at my *new* job!! As I brought this request to my new 'Boss', he <u>agreed to let me do it!!</u>

Still not very world – wise, I was nervous but excited as I purchased a Eu-rail pass, which would allow me to travel freely on Europe's train system, with my friend. And a German High School Teacher got airplane tickets for us to fly both to and from Frankfort. She joined us for the flights, going to visit her family members who lived there. We had one month to spend travelling!

Our adventures were numerous – too numerous to share, but I continued to learn that it was important for me to identify and share my feelings and needs. Travelling together can bring out the best and worst in a person, and we did have some rough spots! I do remember that as we boarded the plane to return home, I felt as if my sense of empowerment and my world had grown enormously! And I learned that even fairy-tale places (in my mind) had crab grass and mosquitoes!

The principal and pastor in my new setting were very supportive and welcoming. Within weeks of returning, I met other staff, choir members that I would work with as their director, in three separate groups. And my office was located in the parish house with others who served the parish. I soon set up a routine with my new position.

I remember feeling anxious as I wondered if I might meet or not meet a person who would want to date and share his life with me. Would it happen for me? Or would I go on waiting forever? A day came when I went to talk about it with my new Pastor.

After listening to me describe my hopes and fears, he responded. "Do you think that God would call you to marriage, and not have someone there for you to marry?" I had never thought of it that way! What kind of a God did I believe in? It made sense for me to let go of my concerns and choose to trust.

The following summer, I planned to attend a regional workshop for professionals in my area of work. I remember being in a 'desert' period, unlike anything I had yet experienced. My prayer and worship felt absolutely *dry* to me. AND, I felt drawn inward, and was not outgoing. Where was this God that had taken such care of me and my affairs through my job change and move? Why is this happening?

The workshop was a good opportunity to get away and hope for some renewal. I enjoyed the presenter – a nationally known composer – but reached out to very few fellow participants. After a few days, one guy reached out to me. It felt good to share with him where I was at. Yet I soon learned that he was a *married* person. He was a great listener and chose to put his arm over my shoulders as I shared. I had mixed feelings about this, but felt like a sponge, wanting to soak up his affection! He was very clear with himself and me about boundaries; still, we spent hours together sharing, as the workshop allowed. I wondered, "Where could this possibly go?"

Toward the end of the workshop, this new guy friend told me that he had a good friend who was coming to my community for surgery in two weeks! Could he stop in and introduce me to this friend? "Yeah, sure," I thought. "I wonder if he will really follow up on this."

But, two weeks later, I received a phone call from him! I was asked if he could pick me up to visit his friend, who was already in the hospital! So I went with him. Little did I know what all would follow.

His friend just had a football – sized abscess removed from his side. And, the doctors wanted his incision to heal from the inside – out. He would be in the hospital for some time! Our meeting was a little awkward, because his friend's parents and sister were present. But I felt moved as I saw his friend ask his father about a hospital billing, which he was trying to understand. "He seemed open to receive help... vulnerable", I thought to myself. Shortly, we left.

During the following week, it kept going through my mind that this new guy was in a hospital, about four blocks from my workplace. He knew only a few people in this city... perhaps he would appreciate a visitor. I called to ask – and my visit was welcomed. As I got to know him, I learned that he too had been through a period of emptiness. His home town doctors suspected that he had Crohn's Disease, a life-long ailment. This friend desired marriage, but had been wrestling with the thought of bringing anyone into his life with such an illness.

As his abscess was removed, doctors realized that he did *not* have Crohn's and gave him that information. Suddenly his 'life sentence' was being released! I visited him, and he always made sure to invite me to return! Our relationship took shape slowly.

Five weeks later, this guy had recovered enough not to need in-hospital care. His incision was healing nicely. (I learned later that they 'put him under' to change the dressing in his wound for the first week!)

In my heart, I knew that I needed to let go and see if this relationship would go anywhere. I waited.

Two weeks later, my workshop friend called me to ask if I had received 'the letter' from his friend! *The* letter? I hadn't received anything! I waited yet another *two weeks* before a thick envelope was delivered to my place of work; *sent to the wrong address!*

Yes indeed, this new relationship would continue. Our friendship grew slowly. My new boyfriend dealt with me as a friend – and was not affectionate for the first three months of our relationship. Like me, he didn't have a lot of experience with dating. I appreciated but didn't always like his caution!

We soon established a rhythm of 'his coming down' or 'my going up' to spend time with each other. We lived two and one quarter hours apart.

When I went 'up,' we would spend time together. Then in the late evening, I was welcomed to sleep in the home of my workshop friend. After another long day together, I drove home, often very tired and even nodding off on the way. I used candy and munchies in an attempt to keep myself awake. Thank God I didn't have an accident! When he came 'down', he was welcomed to stay in the rectory where I worked.

Long story short, we were engaged in one year. I happen to notice numbers and realized that I met my fiancé on 7/22/77, after my 27th birthday in room 7-222 in the hospital! And he proposed on 7/28/78 after my 28th birthday! I certainly could not have lined up something like that!

Zoom ahead two years and you would find us married and living in a small starter home, in the same community.

I had continued to find some weight loss by dieting. In fact, I liked the Weight Watchers Program© and kept coming to their doors. My struggle was that I could not stay on an eating plan; I would be a member for weeks, days, or even hours. My inability to succeed or stay on track was a source of frustration for me. Secretly, I felt ashamed. My dream was to feel good about myself and my body, and losing weight became my obsession as to how I might achieve that.

One day, when we were both home, I decided to 'stay on track' no matter what! By mid-afternoon, I was going 'mad' with my inner craving for sugars and carbohydrates. I cried and told my husband that I didn't know what to do!

His response to me was "I don't know how to help you either. Please get help." So I prayed to be led. I didn't know, either, what I needed.

Within the week, I went to meet with a Clergyman, who was a recovering alcoholic.

"You need to get yourself to Overeater's Anonymous (a sister program of Alcoholics Anonymous for people who are compulsive eaters)."

Some days later, he approached me. "Are you getting to meetings?" "No", I replied, for I had a schedule conflict with their meeting time for two weeks. "*This* is more important. Do you want to hide from me when you see me coming? Go." I cleared my conflict and went to my first meeting.

Unlike WW and other programs, I learned in OA that I *couldn't* control my eating. I needed to know that I was powerless over it and needed a Higher Power's help. This clicked with my insides. Because OA was quite new yet, we used the literature of Alcoholics Anonymous and substituted the words "food" for "alcohol". In fact, I was one fourth of the group! I asked one member to be my sponsor and began in earnest.

Part 2

Into Recovery

Chapter 3

Bankruptcy

I knew that OA (Overeater's Anonymous) had answers to the questions that had plagued me about my eating. But, in spite of myself, my intake seemed to get *worse* as I attempted to wrap my mind around this new concept of powerlessness. "If I can't control my eating, why try?" My sponsor met with me to delve into these new concepts.

For several months, I still floundered. I saw, for the first time in my life, that compulsive eating was a vicious cycle for me. I was either dieting or eating freely and saying "The heck with it!" I really desired recovery. And, I started to see the unhealthiness in many of my relationships. Burying my feelings with food no longer served me as a positive way to cope with life. Still I struggled with my compulsion.

Six months later, I went once again to my recovering clergy friend. "I'm really struggling", I said. He listened to me for some minutes, and then said to me, "You haven't **claimed spiritual bankruptcy**, have you?" Powerlessness, the foundation of the 12 Steps of recovery is built on knowing that I was physically, emotionally and spiritually bankrupt.

I knew that I was physically bankrupt, for my body had a lifetime of being abused with overeating and dieting. My weight was either going up or coming down.

Emotional bankruptcy was also not difficult for me to claim. For, emotionally, I was either 'high' on life or 'down' on life. I was rarely in-between.

But spiritually bankrupt? Spirituality and religion had been the focus of my life up to that point. For me, spirituality is connected with choices I make and how I live out my values. Religion embraces the beliefs I take on from my church. I believed in God and simply could not imagine how spiritual bankruptcy applied to me.

"Well," my friend continued, "**You won't recover until you do**!!!!" I felt as if I had been hit by a two by four inch board! Leave it to this clergy person to not mince with words!

I left his office trying to wrap my mind around this concept and remember looking up at the dark sky and praying simply "Well, God, I guess I don't know you!"

Beyond my wildest imagination, I felt my entire belief system removed from me at that moment. I perceived a blank sheet inside, upon which a new start would take place. As I look back at this challenge, I feel so much gratitude - that someone could understand what I needed and love me enough to be that honest with me! Without that challenge, I could have gone on floundering for months or years!

What was I letting go of? At that point in my life, God was outside of me and not within me. My image of God was built on what I had been taught, and not on my life experience. My God judged, sometimes harshly (good heavens, look at the God of the Old Testament!). And, God called me to accountability. I didn't know what to do with my feelings such as anger, or with shame. I guess that they were so buried in me that I was hardly aware of them! My spirituality to that point held many 'shoulds'. I was not at peace with myself, and surely not free!! My 'religion' was built on negativity - "Thou shalt not...." In spite of 'being taken care of' many times to that point in my life, my head still held the God of my childhood. But, suddenly, all that was all gone.

I felt a great void inside. Being a good 'do-er', I thought of going to a Bible study to attempt to fill this void. But, again, I was sent the messenger and message that I needed to hear... "We do not control our relationship with God. God will reveal himself or herself to us in his or her time."

So I lived in this void. In time, my experiences started to speak to my heart.

Chapter 4

I hunger.
A gnawing inside
presses me onward
to seek,
to be filled.

For what do I hunger?

I need.
An emptiness inside
moves me to search on
until I am filled.
Sustained.

Fill me, Lord.

I am filled for a time

but again,
just as the fullness
of time shared
or meal eaten
wears away,
a hunger grows inside…

Fill my
empty,
hungry hollow
with food for my journey.

Soothe the ache
of my emptiness;
for,
only in you, Lord,
can I be healed,
satisfied,
filled full.

Chapter 5

Judgment

For some reason, I had a habit of judging people and situations as I grew up. I believe now that it was a way of coping, for my self-concept was not a positive one. I either felt 'high' on myself or 'down' on myself; there was rarely an in-between! And when I felt down on myself, judging others was a way of attempting to feel better than they were, based on comparisons in my mind. It was also a response to my fear that others were judging me! What a vicious circle!

What I didn't know was that my perception of myself and others was distorted and not accurate. My perception was colored by shame, by a belief system that was not free. Slowly, working the twelve steps helped me to clear out some of that distortion, to come into freedom and, I believe, into a more real perception of God, myself and others.

Still, habits do not die easily. It took me many years to begin to let go of judging and understand how limiting this habit was.

I remember one day when I went to a meeting with people I didn't know. One person, in particular, was outfitted in clothes that seemed 'trendy' to me. I certainly wouldn't dress that way! In my head, I put her in a box of judgment; I cannot even remember what the box entailed, but I do know that I was disapproving of her appearance. Wouldn't you know it, of all the people at my meeting, that same gal was the **one** person that reached out to me in a friendly way!

It was clear to me that my thoughts and judgments were inaccurate and limiting. I continued to ask God to help me release this habit.

On another day, I was sharing a 5th step with a young clergyperson. Steps 4 and 5 of the 12 steps encourage me to take a fearless, moral inventory of myself, and then to share it with someone that I could trust, who understood my program. Doing this is not comfortable but important in getting honest with ourselves, and also in learning what it is to be human. I was in the process of doing that when I was told something that I've never forgotten. I must have been sharing some judgments with this person, because he chose to respond in a way that stopped me in my tracks.

He said, "You might want to call one day 'bad' and another day 'good', but how do you not know that the day **you** judge as 'bad' isn't the day that God is working in significant ways in your life?" A ray of clarity came into my being, for I could see that my perception of any day, feeling, person or event was limited. To judge is to carry on as a judge and jury. I do not have the ability to know another's wounds, experiences or motives. AND, I started to learn that not judging freed me to be myself. I could begin to let go of my fear of "what other people think" and begin to experience the freedom of being me! Today, I can honestly say that I like who I am; what a freedom and gift!

Chapter 6

Black and White Thinking

In my younger years, if I didn't like what another person was doing, I wanted to label their actions in a black and white way. Can you see how such thinking leaves the author on the outside? In essence, I was not identifying with this action as one that I was capable of. Or, I was denying traits which were already in me. There is little love in such thinking, either toward myself or towards the other.

Recently, I became aware of a phrase that touched my heart. It was "surrender to the spirit of Love." I had never heard an invitation to surrender put in such a light! This invitation feels quite differently to me than the suggestion that I surrender to God's Will or even simply to surrender. The first invitation brings me to desire surrender! The second and third seem as invitations into unknown places, which can stir up fear in my being.

I remember a turning point in my understanding. I was in depression. And I remember the thought of death as a feeling of relief. Fortunately, I knew that I would not hurt myself, but it was the first time that I could understand the feelings of someone who might consider suicide! My thought was not bad. It was one of suffering! For me, it helped me consider the plight of another with compassion and in a new light. It also helps me as I learn to love myself. I desire such growth!

I come from a place, myself, of wanting things clear, spelled out in black and white. How freeing it is as I learn the ways of compassion and love!

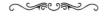

Chapter 7

The Summer of
Stolen Vegetables

My husband and I have gardened almost every year as we created a home together. We had each grown up on farms, and enjoyed planting, weeding, harvesting and preserving fruit and vegetables that we would use for our meals. In fact, my favorite parts were planting, weeding and preserving, and my husband best liked keeping an eye on the harvest, and picking vegetables. For me, working with the soil reminds me of my connectedness to the earth, and weeding was a form of therapy. I took pride in our harvest. And using those canned or frozen vegetables brought me in touch with the golden days of summer and green growing things all year long.

I will admit that some part of gardening had been a 'should' for me. There was enjoyment and renewal in this work, but when we undertook too large a garden, I felt that I was pushing myself to do more than I enjoyed and felt burdened. It took me several years to find a good balance with our choices. During this particular summer, we were yet into gardening on a grand scale.

Two spaces were available to us. One was moderate, and in our own backyard. The second was across the alley from our home, a huge garden space in a widow-neighbor's yard. It seemed like a 'win-win' situation, for not only could we enjoy our own produce; but we could also share with the widow who lived there.

Everything was planted and growing. With all of the space that we had, we could grow vine crops that took extra room…cucumbers, melons and squash. I looked forward to enjoying fresh cantaloupe from our own garden and Roland dreamt of sweet baked squash.

One warm day in August, my husband let me know that some of our vegetables were missing! He knew that we had exactly 13 cantaloupes growing on our plants. But that day, only 9 remained. Also a pepper plant had been uprooted, and two squash were broken from their vine and strewn between the other vegetables. In the days that followed, we learned that another neighbor, good friends of ours who lived two blocks away had their potatoes dug up and stolen!

I wrote in my journal: "Vandalism to our garden – four times already. Stealing, destruction, waste. I feel powerless, and desire to punish this injustice and lack of respect. Each time I have felt my powerlessness, I have tried to let go. But my fear returns – will someone come and vandalize again?"

I felt violated. I grew up without any experiences quite like this one, yet now I needed to face that 'someone' out there was violating our work, property and source of nourishment and pride. I really struggled because I didn't know who was suspect…it could have been anyone! I remember feeling suspicious of almost *everyone*! I didn't choose this feeling, it was just 'there' inside of me. And it was a feeling and reality that I DID NOT LIKE. My anger and fears felt obsessive and permeated my thoughts. I prayed often, asking for help with my feelings and with this situation.

Some days later, my husband went out for a walk, which he enjoys doing. He returned rather quickly, though, and asked me to come with him. Caught up in a project, I hesitated but left what I was doing and followed. Standing on the sidewalk in front our next door neighbor's house, he pointed to the upstairs windows. When I turned my gaze in the direction that he pointed, I saw a set of windows that not only were open, but also had three big cantaloupes sitting in them! The cantaloupes were not quite ripe yet, and our 'neighbors' believed that they would finish ripening in the sun! It didn't take me long to understand. "What should we do?" my husband asked. I thought that we should call the police! "Perhaps we should first call their landlord," my husband suggested. We knew their landlord, and he lived just three houses away.

After we talked with the landlord, he went to the apartment, spoke with its tenants, and reported to us that he also saw a stack of potatoes in one corner! Of course, the renters denied having taken the vegetables. The police were summoned, but by the time they arrived, all 'evidence' had been cleaned up; there was no tell-tale produce to be found.

I was 'miffed'. Not only had these people stolen from us and been destructive to our property, but they also seemed to get by with it!

I remember the weeks and feelings that followed very well. Whenever these particular neighbors hung their laundry outside to dry, a part of me wanted revenge. Maybe I could throw their fresh clothes down on the ground and get even! I had enough recovery in me to know that these thoughts were from my inner child and not thoughts to act on. But what was I to do with such thoughts? I wrote in my journal, "God, I want to see these menacing neighbors punished. And all **You're** going to do is love them!"

I have a spirit that asks a lot of questions. And, slowly, I've learned that if I trust, my questions will eventually be answered. But, at this time, I couldn't fathom what my answer might be!

My desire for revenge continued during the weeks that followed. I was uncomfortable with these feelings, but I was also learning not to judge them. Feelings are not chosen, they *just are*. Recovery, for me, is the ability to identify, accept, feel and deal with them. As I wrote in my journal, weeks later, it came to me that, "…yes, God DOES love those neighbors." As much as I wanted to see them punished, our neighbors **would** have consequences for living with the choices that they made. I did not need to oversee those consequences, mete them out, nor did I even need to understand them. For me, that lesson was the beginning of a spiritual wisdom to "let go". And I began to understand that in His wisdom, God does not punish us, but has put in place laws that are just *and* loving.

Journal Prayer: Thank you, God, for these moments of insight, and for the recovery that you are leading me in.

Chapter 8

Becoming

Can I dare to shed the parts of me that have not been
healthy – and free,
    that have limited and bound me,
    that have kept me from knowing myself and you, God,
    in me?

Help me to release the branches that you have allowed me
to identify which need pruning
    so that I may grow stronger,
    become more free
    and delight in who I am and who you are in me.

You are the God of growth.
No branch or root is wasted in your ecology, even when pruned,
    but is used to reach for good,
    to learn of growing, stretching, becoming.

Even those branches pruned add to the strength of the growth.

Help me to let go Lord, to trust, to become.
Help me to forgive myself for not knowing better
    at each stage of my life.

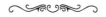

Chapter 9

There Was No Question in My Mind

During the first years of my marriage, I received a letter from a Filipino who asked me to support him through school. I had no idea how he got my name. My husband felt that I should be cautious, but my heart went out to this young man.

His family was poor. Both of his parents were the children of lepers who in the Philippines were sent to an island to live. At that time, lepers received help from the government of the Philippines but assistance was not given to their children. As a result, both of Allen's parents were illiterate. It was Allen's dream to get an education which could open up possibilities for him.

I chose to support him through grade and high school. I considered Allen a 'foster son'; we corresponded regularly, maybe every month or two. He and his family were very grateful for this help. Once every year, I sent them a box of clothing which I was able to get for them at our local clothing shelf.

Requests for additional help came in between my regular support. Many times, I felt in a quandary trying to discern how to respond, because my original support was tithed from my income. How much could I really do for Allen and his family? Could I trust his seemingly sincere requests? They had sent me photographs, which helped me see their faces and how simply they lived, yet my means were limited.

One May, I received a request for $220! Allen's aunt had ear troubles that required surgery. Could I please send them the money so that she could get the help she needed?

Once again, I felt in a dither. I finally decided that I would put this request into God's hands. For one thing, God knew if this need was a genuine one. If $220 would be made available to me, I would gladly send it to Allen for his aunt. I left it at that for about a week.

Within that week, I received a very unusual letter with a request from a party who wished to remain anonymous. This party stated that his correspondence and request were genuine and valid. He was inviting church musicians to play music 'for the glory of God' each Tuesday that summer from twelve noon to one p.m. If they would accept this invitation, he would reimburse them for their time – at $20 each week!

I counted the number of Tuesdays that I was already going to be working that summer in the church where I was serving, and subtracted some days for vacation. I came up with eleven Tuesdays, and you and I know what 11 x $20 is! I responded that I could fill this invitation eleven times. This person was true to his word, as was I. His prompt check for $220 was sent on to the Philippines to help Allen's aunt.

Oh yes; after corresponding with Allen for about four years, he wrote me a letter saying, "I've never told you this, but Allen isn't my real name, it's my nickname. I was baptized Rolando (which is my husband's first name, in Allen's language)!!!

Chapter 10

My Growing Pains and Depression

My coming into recovery at 30 really brought me in touch with different 'voices' in me. Some wanted to justify eating, some wanted to shame and judge me, others wanted to be 'good'. I found it difficult to know which voices to listen to, and which to trust. Yet recovery told me that I needed to listen within. I had a real mess to sort out! The 12 Steps started to help me discern which voices to listen to, which I needed to 'own' but <u>not</u> follow – and consider which brought new freedom. Slowly, my healthier-self grew – my destructive, out-of-control-self faded.

In my marriage and in my recovery, I was learning that **all** of me is loveable and real and not to be judged. Slowly, ever so slowly that idea grew in me. It was in my head, even though I had doubts <u>long</u> before it could begin to grow in my heart.

At age 34, with much stress and with many difficult life events going on, I went into depression. I finally got help for my depression – but not before I understood how suicidal thoughts and death wishes might be appealing to people at times. And suicide, death felt like the only way out of my ominous, heavy, burdened days. I have had several depressions since that time – some for as long as 14 months. Even <u>with</u> anti-depressants, I've continued to have periods of depression – often months long. I have tried, with my psychiatrist's guidance, to come off of my meds several times. It has not worked for me. In fact, I have had need to increase my dose twice to find more stability in the last fourteen years. When I am depressed, the best way I can describe my thinking is to call it distorted. I have no hope, only despair. And my heavy spirit feels burdened – something I cannot escape. Things that are good for me – like socializing or getting physical exercise are the last things I want to do. Yet my husband, friends and self-prod me to get out or to walk or be with my family when I really don't want to. I'd rather 'hide out' and isolate. I do amuse myself with word or card games – always alone – to get away from my feeling self and into my head more. Or, I read; I love to read. When I am in depression, I have never been able to have a good eating program. I always find myself reaching for carbohydrates to try to soothe myself or elevate my mood. At those times, I cannot trust voices within to make good choices for me. Reaching out, playing music, doing tasks is WORK. And they don't feel good or like a gift to me. How could they possibly be good for anyone else?

I have also dealt with long periods of what I call a spiritual desert. I've come to see these as different from depression. Sometimes, I have years where my profession will not touch my own soul and God seems to have left my insides dry. I appreciate but do not believe positive feedback given at work. My creative self feels dead. Yet I need to press on to function, to know my limits, how much I can handle. But, oh, I'd much rather feel alive than like a walking empty person. Yet I cannot change this place when I am there. I doubt my gifts. I feel emptied and find less meaning in my life and spirituality. But I have come to realize that periods

Chapter 11

Emptiness

How low can this get?
I'm afraid – it's so
black in here and
I'm still going down.
I don't know how
to hope or dream
anymore...the
very things I had
come to hope in,
dream, and the God
I believed in feel
gone and empty.
What is my life about?
I am empty of dreams.
I feel barren,
lifeless, like
winter.

Chapter 12

Depression

Feelings press in on me as if I were
wearing a tight, heavy cloak.
What are they about...I wonder...have I strayed
from my path?
I am drawn to a book about suffering and healing.
As I read, I identify several basic human needs
which have been the source of emptiness in me...
the need to be acknowledged by others (and believe them
when they affirm me!),
the need to know that I matter,
the need to express myself freely,
and the need to be loved unconditionally.
As a peacemaker who hid her own feelings in my family,
I know my pain,
but this book helps me to put my needs into words.
This book also speaks of unexpressed grief
becoming a deep, lasting wound.
Reading that has helped me to realize
the source of my heaviness.
Last summer, I identified and released shame that I
experienced growing up.
And this summer, I am realizing how fear has kept me
from living freely.
Asking to release this chain that has limited me
and kept me bound,

I have hoped to walk in a new freedom, a new beginning.
Yet, I live in a void, with a kind of meaninglessness
in my days.
Now I know that I need to grieve before I can heal.
Father of light, love and healing,
I bring you these wounds in my being.
I long to be made whole and to learn who I can be.
I may always carry battle scars…
that help my heart be one of compassion…
But too, they will become a part of my strength
and gift to share.
Father, God of consolation, help me to mourn
so that I may shed this cloak and walk through this storm.
With all my being, I thank you!

Chapter 13

Honesty

I once taught with a woman who prided herself on her honesty. "I'm very honest, maybe too honest!" she would say. Her honesty was difficult to hear, for she would share exactly what she thought about something or someone. Her words were often critical and hurtful. Only years later did I learn what honesty truly is. It was in recovery that I came to understand that honesty is not telling you what **I** think about **you**; honesty is telling you **who I am and how I feel**! My honesty may not always be comfortable, but it is always freeing. It took time for me to learn to honor myself.

Another piece of recovery, for me, was looking at 'rigorous' honesty. I grew up being a basically honest person and valued that trait in myself and others. However, there were little areas where I would not be rigorously honest. I was told once by a family member, "Don't claim your side incomes at tax time…the government gets plenty in taxes!" For me, side incomes included having several piano students whose parents might pay on a 'per lesson' or 'per month' basis. There was no record of this income, unless I chose to keep a record. I also played organ and piano for weddings and funerals. Again, it would be my choice to keep track of that income and choose to claim it, or not to.

Early on in my recovery, I heard 'rigorous' honesty referred to at my 12 Step meetings, but it took a while for that concept to hit home. If I did not claim all of my income, am I being truly honest? I wanted to get healthier, that was clear to me. So, I started to clean up my act and claim all of my income.

Another area that needed work in my life was being honest with people when a part of me wanted to please them. I grew up with many 'shoulds' about putting others first or exemplary ways to be 'nice'. Growing up, I would battle with myself. I truly may have wanted to say 'no' to someone, but I would tell myself that I was not being kind or loving. What I did not understand was that I was not being kind or loving to myself!

I grew to believe that my honesty – my gut response about a request or involvement – was from my inner guidance; from the part of myself that is God living within. Would I not honor God-in-me *and* myself by being honest with both myself and others?

I had a harsh inner critic, developed from years of self-recrimination telling myself that my honest gut feeling was not okay! Prayer and awareness helped me take little steps to let go of that habit and to realize how freeing it is to honor myself!

I was not comfortable with my honest response for a long time; however, I learned ways to 'own' my honesty and take responsibility for it. Being clear with myself and others became truly freeing! I also began to learn how I would experience *healing* as I started to *'be who I truly was'*. I learned that 'living in the light' involves having *no secrets;* not pretending I am someone I'm not to myself or my God!

I desire, with all my heart, to be a light-bearer in today's world! Being honest has become my choice and practice.

In doing so, I honor myself, my fellow Human Beings and my God!

Chapter 14

My Truth

I cannot cling to my truth…
　　my Truth is living, not to be contained.
I cannot hold on to being well-rested,
　　content after a meal, or
　　　　to people I hold dear and love
　　　　for life moves on,
　　　　has cycles, is to be lived
　　　　but not to be possessed.

I move on, sometimes feeling weary… hungry…
　　empty… mournful for what I cannot hold.

Do I like this? Sometimes, not.
　　But I must live life on life's terms…
　　experience its gamut, stretch to new growth.
I could focus on what I don't like,
　　but that would only bring me to stop
　　　　and for a time, not choose life.
　　Perhaps it's okay to stop and rest
　　　　…to feel disillusioned
　　　　…to be in this place.

I just realized – <u>that</u> is the human condition –
　　<u>not</u> being able to cling –
　　　　but needing to release… <u>everything</u>
　　　　in order to live!

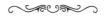

Chapter 15

Coming to Be Myself, Allowing Others to Be Who They Are

There was a time in my life when I was not comfortable if another's feelings and choices were different from mine. This was pointed out to me by a boyfriend! I never know when someone in my life might give me a message that I need to hear! But his saying this made an impression on me.

I didn't exactly enjoy hearing this but it was done in a kind way, and it was accurate!

Why would I have a hard time with people being different from me? In time, I came to realize that this part of me was connected with my insecurity. I could not change that habit within me overnight. But it was a good awareness to have.

Zoom ahead into my time of recovery. I had lived with many 'shoulds' and images of what a 'nice' person would be and do. I was not free with all these 'straight jackets' around me. I was being challenged to own who I am and to embrace that. My program called for a fearless moral inventory which was to be written and then shared with someone who understood our program.

You've hears me say this before, but I really wanted to recover. My first inventory was 16 pages long and took four hours to share!!! I was opening a closet door which had hidden many feelings and thoughts that I was ashamed of and had never shared with another human being.

The outcome was far from what I expected! I realized that I had hid many parts of myself that were simply human… and that I was a human being! And I started to question some of the straight-jackets that I wore which limited my freedom to be myself. I started to realize that I was my worst critic. And many of the 'tapes' I played inside of my head - which affected my choices - were not accurate!

In the beginning it was difficult to know which inner voice to follow in making choices. I had a 'committee' of voices…some judgmental, some fearful, others controlling or hurting. In the past, I would often be paralyzed in fear and indecision! But that was no longer what I wanted.

One by one, I brought these messages to my Higher Power and asked that each be removed. The new Higher Power that I was getting to know wanted health for me and loved me; surely these messages - that divided me against myself – were not my Higher Power's will for me. And when I sincerely asked that a message be removed, it was! The more I did this, the more free I felt to be myself, and desired to be genuine with others.

I had experienced some conditional love, growing up, which was very painful. But now, as I shared who I really was, I was learning that I was not only acceptable, but also loveable!

So changing my approach to life and others greatly challenged my relationships! But, thank God, my husband was working on some of the same things. And, it felt SO GOOD to share with him who I am and find that he wanted to love me unconditionally! There were growing pains in many relationships, but I wanted freedom from my compulsion. And that freedom and clarity grew as I did.

This process was so life-giving that I started to regularly do a 'house-cleaning' inventory and work with these tools that helped me grow! For many years, I felt that 'the older I got, the younger I felt'!! The insecurities of my earlier life faded as I worked with these principles.

Many years later, a new understanding freed me even further in wanting to allow the people around me to be who they were.

I started to think of my time on earth as that of being a pupil in 'earth school'. Like everyone else, I am here to grow. I believe that we take with us – after life – our growth, emotionally and spiritually. And I believe that we are all on similar paths.

One thing about earth school is that we are each at different levels of growth, but learning in the same classroom! Why would I expect someone - that may be in first grade - to be focused on the same things that I am? That would make no sense! Each person needs to be him or herself, just as I do!! And I need to be me!! (The truth **does** set us free!)

Another insight that has served me well is to view the drama of another's life as I would view a television show! I believe that each of us is working on the areas of ourselves that life is leading us to work on. I cannot take that lesson away from another; in fact, my interference may hinder them from learning what they need to learn. I certainly can love and support them in their learning!

We are all children of God. Just as we carry our parents and ancestor's DNA, each human being is a part of God. The connection of each individual to God may not seem obvious at times, but it is there!

Chapter 16

Wounded

We can easily forgive a child who is afraid of the dark;
the real tragedy of life is when men are afraid
of the light. – PLATO

Although I know my woundedness,
I have had the courage
and been given the grace to
own,
feel,
attempt to name
and walk through my wounds.
Each is a part of who I am, of my story.
Sometimes, as I've asked to understand
the root of an issue,
I've been given glimpses of other lifetimes.
I can then better understand my struggles
and embrace who I am.

I believe that there is purpose in having
identified these wounds,
for through them, I have met and come to know
a loving, caring, gentle God
who cares about my well-being and wholeness.
I believe that I have found healing
in many of these areas

so that I can stop focusing on myself
and begin to focus on others.

I am grateful!

A nurse-friend has shared with me
that our scar tissue is stronger
than our original skin.
I marvel as I realize that
each scar has become a part of my strength!

Although I always need balance in my life, I've reflected on what I expect of myself. I came from a background knowing that I was good at 'doing'. But I found myself uncomfortable with 'being'.

Chapter 17

Focus / Balance

TO DO	TO BE
I am worthwhile because of what I do.	I am worthwhile.
"I should…"	I choose to…
God asks me to be accountable for the talents, gifts and possessions he has given me.	God wills that I know his love, live in relationship with Him and others. I feel alive being who I am.
I guilt myself. I am isolated. I 'do' according to what is expected or what my needs are.	I choose to live in relationship with others. I feel connected and become aware of ways we are alike.
I am centered on self.	I am less centered on self. God can work through me.
God calls me to produce? My focus is on what I accomplish.	God wills that I not feel alone; I meet God in my fellows.
Conditional love. I feel loved or loveable only under certain conditions. Am I succeeding? Am I pleasing God or others?	I am loved and learn to love myself unconditionally, as a human being, with both strengths and weaknesses.

Chapter 18

Making Amends

One of the Twelve Steps invites us to make amends with those we have wronged. I trusted these 'guides' to help me get healthier in my life, so I started to look at any relationships in which I might have 'unfinished business', or resentments. Resentment was defined as old anger and tells me that something is unresolved for me.

I happened to have a lot of old anger in one family relationship. Growing up, I felt like a little mouse alongside a lioness that could use her anger in an assertive way. So many times, I could list all that had been done **to me** by this family member...I felt controlled, manipulated, unable to stand up for myself. I saw people around me getting into the dynamic; they too were uncomfortable with her anger and asked me to cooperate with things that she wanted. I had a load of unresolved feelings in relating with this one!

But the Twelve Steps invited me to look at **my** wrongs, not at those of the other. I was quite stumped as I tried to sort out my feelings and baggage.

I remembered considering this situation for months! I was surely learning that these steps were leading me to a new freedom, so I prayed for guidance.

Finally, it came to me that **my** part in this situation was that I had simply not been honest with this person...ever! Now, the thought of making this amend was not a fun one, but I desired recovery. In my prayer, I asked for guidance and for a good opportunity to share this. And, sure enough, that opportunity presented itself.

I clearly remember this. After I shared – with this family member – that I had a habit of not being honest with her, I experienced a 'clean sheet', a new beginning in this relationship! My whole load of unresolved feelings evaporated inside of me!

I rejoiced in this newfound freedom! But then it dawned on me – oh, crap – that I needed to be honest with this person from that day forward!

This new habit was built slowly and often without ease or comfort on my part. But this particular person **had** heard what I had shared...and was sensitive to my struggles as I worked on sharing what I really felt. I appreciated that!

Years later, when this person was dying, I rejoiced in the grace and growth that had led me to make that amend, for I truly had no unresolved issues in this relationship. Thank God! I truly felt grateful!

Chapter 19

Ongoing Healing and Transformation

Many miracles of healing happened in me as I continued to live in relationship with a loving Higher Power.

One thing that had never been 'sane' for me was the ability to discipline myself in several areas. I learned in my program material that impulsive people and addicts have little ability to incorporate self – discipline into their daily lives. I grew up taking piano lessons (and later organ lessons) for over ten years, yet never had the ability to practice my instrument daily. I had the best of intentions, but inevitably would go at it sporadically, cramming at the end of the week before my lesson!

I chose music as my area of study and continued piano and organ lessons through my college years and worked at getting a regular practice in, though not always successfully.

Some years later, as I was working in my career, I came to a time when 'my well had run dry' and I really disliked my work. I considered changing fields for a time...but finally an insight spoke to my dilemma. What I realized was that my professional work had become mostly 'out-put' with little 'in-put'. I felt isolated, having little contact with others in my field. With that came the awareness that I could make changes which would deal with these areas of need. I sought a professional from whom I could take organ lessons, for playing organ was one area that I was simply hating.

I searched out a Methodist minister who was willing to teach me. He had one requirement that he asked of me. Besides charging a professional fee, he asked that I practice one hour each day while I studied with him!

Now, I carried much shame for not having the ability to discipline these parts of my life. And my program was giving me opportunities to deal with these feelings. What I was learning was that my Higher Power could bring 'sanity' to my life when I made a plan of what I desired to do, knowing fully that I could not carry it out by myself, and then asked my Higher Power to help me follow through with my plan. These steps had aided me in dealing with food – would they not work with organ lessons?

I made my plan,' turned it over', and practiced as I was asked – one hour each day for the year and one-half that I studied under this minister!

I was delighted as I came back to loving my profession. And, I had developed a new technique that brought new life to my playing. Ever since that time, I make it a point to challenge myself to learn new pieces regularly and to connect with others who do the work I do.

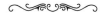

Chapter 20

More Growing Pains

I have never seen pain as a positive experience. I believe that it is natural to avoid painful situations or to choose what options I feel would cause me less pain.

My use of food became my attempt to escape feelings and situations that were uncomfortable for me. It was also an attempt to nurture myself and lift my mood. It was my way of coping with life. Yet in time this habit had become an unhealthy compulsion.

Recovery gave me the opportunity to look at all of me as I am. Of course, I had parts of myself that I liked; I knew how to please a lot of people! But there were other parts that I buried in my eating, parts about which I felt shame and parts that were hidden – even to me!

I've heard it said that if we bury our feelings, we bury <u>all</u> of them. We cannot pick and choose which feelings we want to bury. And, memories are built on feelings. Unlocking our feelings also unlocks our memories.

I was amazed as I freed up and felt more feelings, how many memories came back to me! These 'replays' felt as if I had experienced the event yesterday, not years ago!

The 12 Steps may not be for everyone, but for me, they gave me a framework within which I could break down my recovery into workable steps. And, I also had a support network of people who understood, and needed me as much as I needed them. I *worked* the steps. I really desired recovery. I felt sad when I witnessed others who came to our program and seemed not to delve in, missing the benefits that could be theirs. For me, my years in the 12 Steps held much healing and many miracles!

I would not have grown without moving out of my cycle of overeating and denial. It was a huge awakening when I started to see my life with new eyes – as it truly was!

As I grew to embrace all of me, I couldn't help but see how real my self-concept was becoming. Yet, not everything about myself was 'comfortable'. But, the truth was setting me free!! I learned not to judge my emotions. As I shared, emotions are not chosen – they just are. And they help me learn about myself.

I learned that I had a conscience that served me as a guide. Yes, some of the shame I felt helped me realize that I could be very judgmental toward myself! I also grew to realize that I felt shame whenever I overate, for I felt that I should be able to control my overeating. But I couldn't. And some of my shame was built on distorted thinking and messages that I had been given by others.

I learned to ask for help. Both spiritually and physically, I was not alone. I had a fellowship of friends who understood my struggles. Asking opens a window of willingness to receive help from a vast seen and unseen world. By doing so, I am admitting that I cannot grow by myself – good heavens, I had tried to overcome parts of myself over and over before recovery! And, I am a spiritual being as well as a human being. How can I know what helps are available to me unless I ask?

Anger was a hard emotion for me. I had it so buried that I believed that I never felt it! Uncovering my anger – in layers – allowed me to see situations in which I felt violated. I also learned – from my husband – that my anger is my friend! To me it felt messy as I started trying to deal with this emotion. I felt that sharing that I felt anger with another would send most people wanting to escape my presence! But anger did help me to stand up for myself! It took time to learn ways to 'stand up for myself' without announcing that I felt anger! And, it took time to realize that those who really valued me also valued my honesty.

Recovery, I learned, takes us back to the age that we were when we started 'stuffing our feelings'. When my husband and I started to own our anger, we did a lot of screaming, not unlike two six year olds! I'm sure that our neighbors, hearing our loud screaming, wouldn't have bet a nickel that our marriage was going to stay intact for long! But, one year later, we were able to share our anger sitting at our table and talking in normal speaking voices! It takes what it takes. We were both committed to recovery!

I had the inclination in myself to want to strike out, physically, as I tried to share anger with my husband. But we soon established a 'no hit' rule between us. I feel that this was connected with how powerless I felt in the face of this powerful emotion. And, I did have a scapegoat for my anger in a sibling, as I grew up. I needed to ask for forgiveness and to forgive myself for that! It took time to learn I could be my own friend and that I was worth standing up for. And, I learned that words *do* have power.

Another emotion that I found very uncomfortable was the feeling of attraction to someone, after I was married.

I have worked for churches during most of my professional life. My commitment to feel my feelings was growing stronger at this time in my life. I developed an attraction to a priest that I was working with. What could I do with that? I simply remember the strength of my feelings and obsession, and **not knowing how to deal with them**!

Step two of the 12 steps states "Came to believe that a power greater than ourselves could restore us to sanity." So, for a long time, I prayed that God restore sanity and peace to my inner self! Yet, weeks became months. One day, I decided to risk sharing my struggle with my husband. Now, this may not be the way to go with just any husband, but my husband was also working on his emotional health and recovery from unhealthy ways. And, I knew that freedom could come from my 'not keeping secrets' and sharing with another.

I do not remember what day it was, or even what season, but I do remember the feeling of that experience and where I sat! I shared how afraid I was of this powerful feeling of attraction. My husband replied simply, "You don't trust yourself with that feeling? I trust you!"

I felt stunned! Before this, I had been asking God to **remove** this feeling. Perhaps I needed to allow it to become a part of the fullness of emotion that I felt as a human being! Could I trust myself with these emotions?

In time, I came to see that my attraction to this priest affirmed my attraction to my husband, for they had many qualities in common. And, my inner life felt much more peaceful! Thank God for growth, and learning about being 'fully human, fully alive'!

The following summer, my husband felt 'crazy' with his feelings of attraction to an intern that he was working with. My experience just months before blessed my ability to let

Chapter 21

With New Eyes

Lord, you are helping me see so many things in
a new light these days...and I am grateful for that.
You have helped me to see that life is not limited
to just my experience of it...
and you are not only who I
(with limited perception) perceive you to be
I need to keep an open mind and heart to
others' experiences of life and relationships with you.
I find myself knowing intensely my need
to reach out of myself and grow in relationship
with others and with life.
I need to be more involved with life.
I'm coming to learn that your will
is not centered in what I do,
but more so in my being and reaching out...
bringing who I am and affecting how I live.
I'm also coming to learn
that I need to take responsibility for my life
and yet learn to surrender to the 'things I cannot change'.
So many things, Lord, are making a lot of sense to me.
Yet, I need your help to make them a reality.
Please help me to grow, Lord.

Chapter 22

Re-birth of My Beliefs

My image of God formed slowly as I reflected on experiences I was having. Yet, my first impressions needed again to be released several times.

After our first son was born, I found myself overwhelmed. A beautiful baby, he became a high energy toddler who was very verbal. I'd ask him, "Aaron, do you want peas or green beans for lunch? Inevitably, he would ask for an entirely different option than I offered. I had been parented by mom who used praise and at times guilt when she was not happy with me. (I'm not putting mom down; we each use the tools we have available to us.) Yet if I tried to control Aaron in any way, my attempts were futile! I really struggled as a new parent.

It was years before I realized that I was stuck in post-partum depression. I sought help and was put on medication. In time and with help my parenting skills grew.

Life happenings contributed to the tumult of those years of raising my toddler, for my Mom battled with cancer. And I had two surgeries on my left ear. Still I had the desire growing in me for a second child. Being one–sixth of my Mom's children brought me enrichment and a great comfort at the time of her death and I wanted that kind of relationship for our son. We kept the door open to that possibility.

This kept me on the roller coaster ride of hoping and praying, waiting, and then having my hopes dashed each month.

Now, I did believe that my desire for another child was God-given. Yet why would I conceive, only to lose that pregnancy in miscarriage? I believed that new life was from God. The image that was forming for me, at that time, was of a supreme power pulling at my strings – like a puppeteer, only to yank from me the focus of my desire. After all, wasn't God 'in control'? This image disturbed me. Was this the God that I believed in? I chose to claim spiritual bankruptcy a second time.

My compulsive overeating went up and down during the following months, as I struggled with soul-questions. Why did my Mom die, after the doctors believed that they had eliminated her cancer, only to have it return with a vengeance? Why was I led to surgery of my inner ear and given the hope that it might restore my hearing in that ear, which had left me three years previously? I needed to wait 6 months before I could know the surgery's outcome, only to find that it had failed. And why was I given the desire to have another child, only to have my hopes dashed twice in miscarriage? Although I went into depression, I wanted answers.

One day, I came upon a book which spoke to my heart. It was "Embraced By the Light" by Betty Eadie. In it, Betty described her experience of death after surgery in a hospital and shared a detailed account of what she learned on the other side. Betty was brought back to this life with the mission of sharing this experience.

I was hungry to know about such things and read it in wonder.

I learned that often 'great' souls, who are advanced in their growth choose to come into their life on earth with handicaps, in order to help their loved ones grow in love and service. When I read that section, we were vacationing at a lake resort. As I went to the playground to watch my son play, I noticed a little girl wearing leg braces and walking awkwardly among the other children present. I thought to myself, "**There** is a **great soul**!" I stood in wonder as the girl moved across the playground, came to me and flung her arms around my legs, giving me a big bear-hug!! Amazed, I wondered if she knew what I was thinking!

I read that God doesn't control. It was shared that we – before birth – choose many of the circumstances of our life in order to grow. Our desire is soul-growth. Some souls would lovingly choose to be conceived, even to be lost in miscarriage, for the soul-growth of those affected. This resonated with me. It was as if pieces of a puzzle were coming together to give me new clarity. Wasn't the God I believed in loving and supportive? If I made these choices for my soul – growth, then let's get a grip and move on! I did just that, yet one thing held me back.

As much as I desired a child, I was terrified of experiencing again the trauma of labor and birth. My first birth had been described as a 'normal vaginal delivery' in my records, yet it took me to a threshold of pain that I didn't know I could live through. I was stuck in the last phase of labor for 9 hours before the doctor used a 'high' forceps to help our son come through. He had given me only Demerol for pain.

I wanted to be more at peace about this and sought out an obstetrics doctor to help me. After hearing my story, the doctor chose to x-ray my bone structure. Sure enough, the x-rays revealed that my baby had been stuck in me! My bone structure on the inside was borderline – narrow; this doctor recommended a C-section if we had another child. I went home much relieved. *That* felt manageable to me!

Four months later, when our second son was conceived, my desire for answers lessened. In fact, I realized that I did not need answers to the questions that had been burning in my heart. Although hopes had been dashed, my life held goodness and guidance. And my Mom was free of her illness and fears.

I shared this with my spiritual mentor and she suggested that I ritualize my letting go of these questions by buying a helium balloon and going to a park to release it.

I bought the ugliest color of balloon that I could find and prepared for this ritual. Amazingly, as the balloon filled with helium, it clarified its' color as blood red. How fitting!

I drove to the park I was guided to visit and felt overcome with mourning. I found a quiet space and, when I was finally ready, told God ..."I wanted to understand these things but I don't. I choose to let go of my need to know these answers, and to trust." I released the balloon and felt a lightness of spirit. I went on to have an effortless abstinence in my program for seven months!

I carried this baby to full term. His name is Joel; he is a delight and his birth *was* very manageable for me. My family felt complete!

Some months later, I had a dream that really spoke to my heart:

> *In a monastery, I was gathered with my fellow monks. (Yes, I was male.) It was Lent and we stood in line, stripped to our waist, waiting to undergo a penance that we practiced. One monk stood holding a whip with shards of metal on its cords; assisting us with this penance, whipping one of us at a time. I came to the front of the line and suddenly ran away shouting "I don't want to do this anymore!" At a distance of maybe 20 feet, I stopped and turned, expecting that I was being pursued. But no one was behind me!!! What came to me was an awesome awareness. Living in relationship with a vengeful God who would be appeased by such penance or expectations was* **self-chosen***!*

For me the dream was affirming of my new growth and direction!

Chapter 23

Uncovering Layers

A dream spoke to me of the process that I was in.

In the dream, I exited a door off the sanctuary of the Parish church I was then serving. A stairway took me downward. Below, I was amazed to find a large area – shaped like a stadium and similar to the church above. But this area was being excavated. It held layer upon layer of information. Each was being gone through carefully, in order to examine whatever clues it held, as by an archaeologist. The layers held much dirt and dust. It was a work in progress.

I found a hallway off the back of this lower church and followed it to several rooms. One held objects which levitated over a table area; I was amazed as I walked around this. Further rooms held the presence and energy of several saints, which I looked into. As I entered several of these rooms, I physically felt a charge of energy, held by the one inside. One saint was Joseph, the foster father of Jesus. And another was a pope, whose name I did not know. However, he wore a golden papal tiara on his head.

I have marveled as I have reflected on this dream many times. There is a burning desire in me to know truth, especially as I am awakening. I liken my re-discovery of what is true to the work of an archaeologist. Piece by piece I've put together a puzzle of clues – in my reading and learning. I can trust my intuition to 'sing out' in excitement, or have new ideas click into place as I put together these discoveries.

I consider what they tell me. Many times, there is value in giving a new idea time. Try it out and see if it fits. Not everything has been an answer for me! After all, we each are at different levels of learning and growth. In the 12 Step program, we had a saying that we closed our meetings with - "take what you like and leave the rest". What a fitting freedom to offer each person!

And I believe that we, humankind, have abilities that we are unaware of...which have gotten buried in our history and conditioning. When Jesus said that his followers would be able to do even greater works than he, I believe that he meant it (John 14:12)! All good works give praise to the Father!

Chapter 24

Understanding My Chest Pain

There were times, during my later 20's and early 30's when I would experience a sharp pain in my chest. It felt to me like heart pain, and I found myself afraid that it involved my heart.

Years earlier, I was examined and wore a 24 hour monitor, ordered by a Mayo Clinic doctor. After examining my test results, this doctor diagnosed my pain as muscular / skeletal. I basically heard that diagnosis as 'lump it and live with it! Still, during each bout, the pain felt heart-related.

I had some bouts with pleurisy (inflammation of the lining of the lungs) and knew what *that* felt like. But this felt different.

During this particular bout, my husband, a nurse, quizzed me..."Does it hurt more when you are exerting yourself? What kind of pain is it?"

I called my doctor who responded, "Go to the emergency room. I'm not able to see you today. They will be able to check you out." So I did just that.

Shortly after, as I was being examined, I felt shame. I knew, intuitively that my heart was not the source of my pain. Of course, the doctors were stumped, unable to find its' source; but they determined that it was probably **not** my heart.

In the name of thoroughness, my doctor followed up with a stress test (to find if exertion brought on pain) among other tests. He met with me after he had the results of this testing. After giving me the results and wondering, he looked at me and asked, "What do *you* think your chest pain is about?" This stunned me, for my doctor was asking *me*!

Later, in the evening, my husband was holding me in bed. He said "Kathy, you have a lot of tools available to you. What do *you* think your chest pain is about?"

The synchronicity of these events hit me like a ton of bricks. I *did* have many tools in my recovery. And I wanted to know. The next day, I posed a request to the *Universe*,... "I don't know what my chest pain is about, but **I want to know**. Please guide me; I'd like answers."

Within a month, I learned about a bio-kinesiologist, located about an hour from our home. She used a therapy which used muscle testing to get answers from ones' body; answers which may not be available in ones' conscious mind. Bio-kinesiology is built on the belief that our bodies do not forget, and they do not lie. I chose to explore.

It was autumn. Colored, falling leaves became snow covered earth, followed by the mud of spring, new growth, and then the fullness of summer. Our sessions became a process of discovery for the next 18 months! Over that time, I learned of and cleared many generational issues that impacted me. I knew that we were succeeding, for I could *feel*, physically and emotionally a sense of lighter, flowing energy in my being. It took time to get answers about my chest pain. But I stayed with the process. What I learned was this: when I was 3 years old, I did not *differentiate* from my mother. I did not establish my own identity, but *stayed within her boundaries*. It was **no wonder** that I had a hard time establishing boundaries with Mom!!! I had always struggled with that.

Don't get me wrong. I loved my mother who had already passed on, but my relationship with her had not always been an easy one. During my years in recovery, I had attempted to create healthy boundaries with her. My bio-kinesiologist had me 'look' at this binding boundary, which I felt was *rope-like*. She had me step out of it and ask my inner child to come and help me bury it. We then created new boundaries – one around my mom and one around me.

As hard as it is to understand all of this, my chest pain subsided and rarely visited me after that! When I do occasionally have chest pain, I have come to believe that I am feeling my fear of moving on - in some way – in my life. All this time, my body had been attempting to let me know that an emotional part of me needed help! I just needed assistance to hear it!

Chapter 25

Disillusionment

From childhood on, I trusted and looked to my church and its clergy to lead my heart and soul to God, salvation, truth. That wasn't hard with kindly and personable pastors. My Mom's spirituality was one of fear, shame and 'shoulds'. I did not question it. I tried it on as a cloak, but was not free within it. It held rights, wrongs, good, bad and judgment. I **did** want to be good. But behind that desire and drive was the belief that I wasn't loveable unless I was perfect!

And as I buried my feelings and need for affection, I grew to believe that perfection was reached by never being angry and by rising above my humanity. Shame arose whenever I failed at this, or couldn't control some part of my life that I thought I should be able to control.

I feel a twinge of sadness as I reflect on the sense I had of God – even as late as my wedding day. My husband–to–be and I were surrounded by a church filled with loving friends and family, yet my concept of God's presence was **outside** of the church, in the beauty of nature! My future husband believed in God's presence within, but my beliefs yet did not.

My world was turned up-side-down when I came into recovery, one year later. It was as if a 'pair of rose-colored glasses' was removed and I was seeing myself and those around me more clearly for the first time. All the feelings and indicators that had tried to speak to me before this started to gush out and fall into place forming a picture which made sense but was not comfortable to look at. I had idolized parts of my life and now saw a new reality, involving a mixture of denial and pain.

My emotional reaction felt overpowering; I wanted to reject the 'blindness' that I had lived with to that point. Yet I learned of 'sincere delusion' at a workshop. It took time to learn to be gentle with myself and others who would not or could not understand my new perspective.

I started to see how my former ways of thinking and living did not bring me freedom. I was living my life 'as I thought I was supposed to be living it'. "And the truth will set you free." Somehow, I had been missing the boat! It wasn't until I 'owned' spiritual bankruptcy and my powerlessness over my compulsive eating that I could begin with a clean slate to learn anew.

Parts of how I had functioned before that time were not very 'sane'. Sanity is the quality of having a sound mind and a sound body. It took time to find and weed out some of my behaviors which did not serve me well.

A pillar of recovery in the twelve steps is "turning our will and life over to the care of God as we understood God." It makes sense to me now how essential it was to "own spiritual bankruptcy" before I could surrender. There was no way that I could fully "turn my will and life" over to a God who was judgmental and punishing, and trust the God of my childhood to lead me to good!

At times I've yet reacted negatively as I hear people around me – and even, sometimes, ministers speak about spirituality including punishment, retribution or hell-fire. At one time, I attended a wedding where the minister told the couple to "put the other person's needs before their own!" Could that possibly be a healthy message for this couple? But I realize now that many of these 'messengers' have been a part of a shame-based belief system as I had and have yet to learn about emotional health and a God that loves unconditionally. Today, instead of reacting with anger, I find myself feeling sad when I yet hear those things.

I myself learned more about unconditional love – especially in my marriage. And, in reading, I learned new concepts and beliefs that brought my heart to sing!

I learned that my heart's desires were God given, planted in me to lead me! I learned that God ALWAYS loves me, no matter what. God 'wills' good for me – not pain, not suffering. My life had held much pain and suffering, especially in my 20's and 30's...I had much to learn and a lot that I needed to release. It took time for me to begin to understand some of the messages that my body tried to give me in my lack of well-being.

Before recovery, I carried all my pains and grievances from the past. I did not have tools with which to recognize and release 'what kept me sick'. It was important to do that 'work' in order to be free of my past. It was also important to fully feel and identify the feelings I had buried before I could release them. It truly was a process that took time.

My insights came gradually. I was learning that I could trust my insides to let me know when something was not healthy for me.

I came to see how I - and others put clergy and other professionals on pedestals, in hopes that they might have answers for those questions or struggles that plague us. We long to find messengers that know what we need. Idolizing involves loving an ideal that we hold and not the reality that is. That keeps our love conditional. But each person and institution is human and has limitations. We are each in the process of growing. I do not deny that some of those very people have been instruments of God in my life, giving me wisdom that I longed to hear. But it was my disillusionment that helped me come back to reality. I see disillusionment as the experience of having some person, ideal or organization fall off a pedestal that I had them on in my mind. It can be a very painful experience, but is an important step in growing toward health and learning to live in reality.

God – within has become the voice I look to for guidance. I've heard that if I'm confused, I'm not yet ready to make a decision. Guidance comes with time and sometimes in ways we don't expect. But it always comes!

Chapter 26

Who is Jesus?

For many years, I have felt sorrow and guilt about the fact that Jesus suffered and died such a horrific death at the hands of humanity. I knew some about his life and teachings from my teachers and from hearing the Gospels, but still his words and story seemed to hold mixed messages for me. I did not find it easy to relate with him in prayer.

I felt shame as his suffering and death were focused on by some of my teachers and some of the preachers I would hear.

I do not deny that Jesus greatly loved us and suffered. But in time, I began to realize that it was unhealthy for me to focus on the horror of His passion; why not, instead, celebrate his messages and love, the wonder and gift of his Resurrection and all that I've learned from Him? To me, it felt akin to experiencing a difficult labor and birth, and then reminding one's child endlessly of all that one had gone through! There is a time to release pain and our experiences, and focus on the gifts and new life that they hold!

I have heard Jesus' words used to shame. His way has been taught to me with many 'shoulds'. Lent, behavior in church, hell, the evil one, and messages about sexuality have been distorted by some of those who have taught me. I cannot know the motives or issues of those who have given me such distortion, but I feel that religion and God was fearful to them. They were giving me what they had been given. Or, like a fearful parent, they may have not wanted me to go astray. If God lives within each of us and guides us, I need to learn to listen to his voice within and grow up spiritually, not stay a child!

I felt encouraged to suppress my feelings, and 'do the Christian thing' growing up. I found little freedom in that! In recovery, I came to learn that it is important to be honest with myself and others and honor my feelings. I grew to believe that God - within - me was linked with my honesty and that I needed to be true to where I was at in my growth. 'Should-ing' myself did not honor who I was, or where I was at…it kept me divided inside. If the truth sets us free, it surely involves honesty and being who I am! Before that, my love for self and others was conditional. Oh, the freedom of experiencing and giving unconditional love!

Is sin 'being bad', or is it ignoring that we have a soul, a conscience, a Higher Power? I've come to believe that 'sin' is living in distortion and untruth. Our beliefs and actions do hold consequences and limitations for us. Living with inner dividedness distorts our perception of ourselves, others and God. Can there be peace in such a place? I think not. Unfinished business burdened my soul, as did 'not speaking my truth'.

Many times I do not even know the burdens or distortions that we have been born into as we come into human form. I've learned that it's important to 'own' that I have been limited and impacted by these burdens and distortions. I could not shed them alone. I needed a Savior, but not a shaming one!

In my journal, I found a prayer that speaks of my journey in this area.

"Jesus, if God is love, who are you, really? I don't believe that you are all the things which have been told me, in your name. I want to meet the real you. I believe that you are someone much more beautiful and loving than I have been taught. Yet, the things I have been taught stand as a shield and keep me from knowing you. God, help me to break through this shield, bury it, and shed the distortion and lies that it has held for me. I do want to live in truth, and not distortion."

Spiritual bankruptcy opened this door for me. I realized later that letting go of my former beliefs gave me the opportunity to learn anew. And the process that followed this gift has involved 'owning who I am', embracing my feelings as I became aware of them, forgiving myself and others, and a lot of letting go! It certainly didn't happen overnight. But I knew that I was heading in the direction I wanted to go! I also wanted a new relationship with my inner self, Jesus and my Higher Power. And in time that relationship took root and grew.

Chapter 27

The Power of Forgiveness

If you choose not to forgive, it is as if you drink the poison
And you expect the other person to die!
– Author Unknown

A journey into unknowing, I follow my heart.
I am guided one step, one day at a time.
How could I have known the lessons ahead, and the gifts
they would hold?
Merciful, Loving God...you led me to amazing places,
freedom and truths.
I thank you from the bottom of my heart!

I had no idea of the 'secrets' my Mom held in her heart.
She was a loving, kind woman who gave herself to never-ending work and her family. Yet as I grew, I came to be
aware of some of her fears and obsessions. I really didn't
understand where they came from.

When I was in my 'teens', I was given negative messages
about our physical bodies and about men's sexuality. Yet my
father was gentle and loving; these messages just didn't make
sense to me. Later, when I was a single adult, I would receive
newspaper clippings from her about accidents involving
drunken drivers from the area, along with her weekly letter.
I could tell that Mom carried a lot of fears. And telling her
not to worry seemed futile.

In fact, my eyes were opened to myself, my family and life in ways that I could not have predicted…all with my choice to trust the path of recovery. I began to see patterns, interactions and beliefs with new eyes and new understanding. Those first steps were not comfortable or easy, yet I found myself wanting to know more. "The truth will set you free" became the foundation of a new and growing desire in my life.

Some years later, I found myself having dreams about my mother's father, who had died when I was fourteen. Believing that my dreams reflect my inner journey, I wanted to learn about their message to me. Following is a dream that especially spoke to my heart:

> *I dreamt that I watched as loved ones encircled Grandpa and reverently kissed him goodbye. He sat in a chair in the kitchen of his home; all present knew that he was going to die. I had the sense that this ceremony wasn't new, but had taken place through many generations in his family. The parting was very solemn. My Dad, Brother Al and I stood in the dining room of his home, looking on. It was our task to choose which- among several evergreen boughs- would best honor Grandpa at his wake and funeral. My brother chose a bough that was mine, saying "This one is the best. Your tree would best honor him. I thought to myself, "Oh Al; you don't realize that I don't just have a tree on hand! I'll need to search and work to get it."*

I had idolized this particular Grandfather all my life. He was a man gifted in ways that I have been gifted. A skilled musician, my mother would often say that "Grandpa could play any instrument you gave him". I had already struggled to accept the information shared with me in my later teens when my sister told me that Grandpa had a drinking problem. It would be more than ten years after that before I came into recovery.

A part of me wanted to unearth more information about Mom's child-hood. I heard only once (from Mom) that she and some siblings would hide under the table in their home when their Dad came home intoxicated, fearful of his angry mood. But Mom's motto was 'let bygones be bygones'; it was difficult to learn any more. I could not speak to her brothers or sisters; they were unable to own that their father had a drinking problem. But I had a few cousins that were open to my questions. For that, I was grateful.

I struggled with my own compulsions, and was challenged to come into recovery some years later. I worked those twelve steps with focus. I wanted sanity with my eating and freedom from an addiction that impacted me in ways I couldn't have known at first. With time and hard work, I started to experience a new freedom with myself and others. I read of a suggestion - that I write a letter to Grandpa, even though he was no longer living. I did that and wish to share a part of it here.

"Grandpa; I feel sad that your bondage kept me – and probably others – from knowing you better. I know that you were gifted, yet I also know how addiction keeps us from 'owning' our gifts, resulting in a lot of guilt tied in with them and keeps us feeling so inadequate, in spite of our giftedness. I've wondered – who have you been, on the inside? I know that you went to church regularly. Who was God to you? And what was life like for you?

I may never come to answers in my wonderings. Yet, in some way I can feel that I know you a bit – from the inside out. And I know that I am being given a gift in recovery…I hope to pass it on. Maybe, by doing so, I can bring God's healing and honor to a family line that has known emotional pain and sickness".

I sought a spiritual mentor about this time. I was in my thirties when my first child was born, and I was feeling overwhelmed and challenged with this new part of my life. I missed having 'space to reflect', which I had valued and enjoyed before this.

In one of our sessions, I shared with her my dream about my Grandfather. She said to me, "You need to go back into that dream and dialogue with your Grandfather. I have a hunch that this dream has a message for you." She told me how to go about doing this. I was to quiet myself, go back into the dream and ask questions of the people who are in it. Then I was to 'let go' and listen; and see what their response might be.

When I first did this, I did not know what to expect. I attempted to speak with several people in the dream, but none would reply! When I turned to my Grandfather, he sat on a stool – maybe eight feet from me, in readiness to listen.

Now, *I didn't* know what I needed to say to Grandpa, so when I was overcome with feelings of rage, I was surprised. I shouted: "How could you hurt someone who looked to you for protection as a parent?" My Grandfather continued to sit in silence.

When I next met with my mentor, I told her what had unfolded. She said to me, "But you aren't finished! You need to go back and dialogue further with him!" Trusting my mentor, I followed through on my 'assignment'.

In our second visit, Grandpa sat about six feet from me. Again, he said nothing. I asked him, "What was your home life like, Grandpa, when you grew up?" I wondered if he might have experienced abuse.

On our third visit, Grandpa sat about four feet away. I said to him, "You and I have a lot in common. We both have dealt with addiction. And, we are both gifted with music." I marveled as these dialogues unfolded and at the feelings that had been buried inside of me. And I continued to meet and process my feelings with my mentor.

The year 1987 was a rugged one for me. In March, I had ear surgery performed by a Mayo Clinic Doctor, in hopes that freeing the bones in my inner ear might restore my hearing. And I would not know its' result for six months.

At that same time, my Mother was receiving chemotherapy for lymphoma. Lymphoma is an aggressive cancer, yet it responds well to chemotherapy, which gave us much hope. Her cancer had been diagnosed about seven months earlier. The thought of losing Mom was shattering for me. I felt very connected to her though not always in healthy ways. And I could not imagine my life without her.

Being one of six children, I was grateful to not be alone in this ordeal. In May of that year, Doctors told us that they believed Mom's treatments were successful! They wished to give her **one** more round of chemotherapy just in case any undetected cells were yet alive.

Mom never received that treatment. Instead, she developed a fungal infection in her blood, which delayed chemotherapy; the doctors needed to work on clearing this infection. Her cancer returned and Mom died one month later.

Beyond my comprehension, I felt buoyed during the days ahead. The support and grace that I needed were there for me. I couldn't have imagined before this that I would actually feel on a spiritual 'high' through the month that followed! The experiences of Mom's death, wake and funeral were sacred for me. Over a month later, I felt placed back into the reality of mourning.

Some weeks later, my husband, son and I went to visit a cousin who lived some distance away - for a small vacation. The first night, as I slept in this cousin's home, I had another dream about my Grandfather. In this dream, Grandpa sat in a breakfast nook with a window behind him, bathed by the morning light. On the table in front of him lay a piece of paper on which he was writing a letter to me. I awoke from that dream, and knew what my mentor would suggest.

I took some time during that day to quiet myself and go back into that dream. Once there, I asked my Grandfather what he had written. These are the words that came to me...

"Dear Granddaughter, you and I have much in common... our gifts with which we can glorify God...our struggles. I am happy that you have been given the gift and chance to recover. I wish for you health and happiness.

Yes, I have made mistakes and had my weaknesses. The good God has forgiven me for my transgressions."

(Me): "Are you happy?"

"I am happy. Your Mom, she is finally free. I am glad that she will suffer no more. I am glad to see her."

(Me): "God has forgiven you. If God has forgiven you, what sense does it make for me to hold anger toward you? Mom is no longer bound by her wounds and fears. Grandpa, **I forgive you**!" Surprised, but at peace, I broke down in tears. I could not have anticipated this message. And I came to realize, in the weeks that followed, that knowing any more details about my Mom's childhood held no meaning for me anymore. I knew that Mom was free.

As leaves began to turn color that fall, I returned for my follow-up appointment at Mayo Clinic. The plug was removed from my ear – and it was determined that this surgery hadn't helped my hearing. My options were to live with my hearing as it was, or to consider purchasing a hearing aid. I chose the latter; the aid is helpful for me.

In the seasons that followed, I was grateful for dreams in which my Mother came to spend time with me, and let me know that she was happy. When I was 'in' these dreams, I often found myself puzzling why we had believed Mom to be dead, when she was very much alive!

My spirituality continued to be enriched in so many ways because of my reading and a friend's gift of clairvoyance. Though some people have reservations about this gift, I had no doubt that it was genuine. Messages and words that flowed from 'the other side' were always loving, and encouraging; they spoke to my heart.

One thing that I learned was that spirits who have passed on manifest only if they are ready and choose to. They do not sit on a cloud playing a harp with the angels, but continue to learn and be involved with us, each other and life – in ways that are helpful. This was brought home to me in dreams that I would have which included my ancestors.

In one such dream, I came through an area of my parent's home which held a large tapestry of my grandparents of many generations before them. Many wore wedding garb, and several were posed in ways that suggested their being caught up in activity. When I came back through that same room in my dream, I noticed that some of my ancestors were missing from the tapestry, and others had changed position! This observation spoke to me of their being active in their afterlife.

In another dream, I was with ancestors in a dark basement area. I chose to turn on a 60 watt light bulb, which gave us all a dim light. I also saw that with us was a collection of newspaper articles about their lives. In this dream, I saw my mother, just as I was moving to climb a stairway back into my life. She was young. I felt her love for me. Again, I could tell that my ancestors were very connected with each other and myself!

During one summer, my friend came to visit me. I remember sitting at our dining-room table, having coffee with her when a branch came loose and swung from a hanging plant that was near us. "Someone's here," she said. I waited, knowing that an adventure would unfold. She focused inward and told me "It's your Grandpa. He wants you to know that he appreciates the work you have done, connected with him. It has been of help to him." I pondered his words and this visit many times in the weeks that followed. It was a new awareness for me that working through *my* unresolved feelings and forgiveness was helpful to my loved ones – even on the other side.

Another summer, as I spent time with family and friends, I slept in a room with my clairvoyant friend. We were like two kids chattering with the lights turned out; it took us a while to quiet down! When we did, I could sense a spirit's presence. My friend shared with me that first my Mom was present, wanting to speak to us. Later, my Grandpa and his parents came, together. They wanted to let me know that the work I had done was very helpful to each of them. Again, I marveled and felt gratitude that I had been led through my feelings and into forgiveness. I started to believe that generations were impacted by our woundedness. I also realized that generations were freed by our forgiveness.

My Mom has been gone for some time, now. I am grateful for the gifts that recovery has brought to me. My life holds much peace. My awareness continues to be expanded as I read and reflect. I want to include one last message that came to me this last summer from Grandpa.

"You and I have always had a connection. You carried my music, and you carried a lot more stuff. You have healed generations - in that process- more than you know. I am grateful for this. When you do healing of generations, it affects all of us on this side."

It isn't that I never heard about forgiveness as I grew up. Regularly, I heard Jesus' challenge to forgive not seven times, but seventy times seven times*. Even in the Lord's Prayer, I prayed often "Forgive us our trespasses as we forgive those who trespass against us". I knew these things in my head. Yet it wasn't until I learned that I would not fully recover without forgiving that I actually chose to forgive. And I haven't stopped! A new freedom and lightness of spirit are its' gifts; I needed to learn the power of forgiveness!

*Matthew 18: 21 - 22

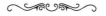

Chapter 28

Reflection on Forgiveness

I've learned that forgiveness is a choice.
Like love, forgiveness cannot be based on our emotions,
but instead must be a conscious choice
to release anger that I would otherwise hold on to.
Anger held for more than a few minutes is considered resentment.
And I've learned enough of life
- in my recovery and healing - that forgiveness frees **my** soul.
An eye for an eye, *'justice'* so fills our thinking and law system
that we don't think twice about the killing of a victimizer
as 'just'.
"He had it coming. It's only fair."
I no longer feel that way.
Often victimizers have been victims also.
They are passing on what they know.
They are not free, not for a minute.
I do believe that there may be exceptions to this
such as a person with no conscience or someone driven by
rage, who sees no options.
But each human being holds a spark of God within.
It may seem hidden, but it's there!
In 'The Lord's prayer', we pray "Forgive us our sins as
we forgive those who sin against us."
I don't know about you, but I grew up hearing and believing
that forgiveness is important.

But I didn't make the choice to forgive until I came into my
recovery, my healing. I had no clue
how my unforgiveness held **me** captive, bound.
I came into a whole new freedom that has been so wonderful
that I don't hesitate to forgive again, and again, and again...
Yes, we likely will need God's grace and help
to come to a place of willingness at times.
But be assured that grace is there for us!
We are led!
Thank you, God, for helping me learn to practice forgiveness.

Part 3

Nuggets of Learning and Wisdom

Chapter 29

Positively

In my earlier recovery, a pamphlet defined abstinence as 'refraining from compulsive overeating **and** from negative thinking'. That definition was a part of my formation in recovery and is still a value I hold in everyday life. That was affirmed by an experience that I had.

In my mid-forties, I had a bike accident and cracked vertebrae in my upper back. I lived with chronic pain, even after my healing was complete. I simply couldn't accept that this was my fate, and pursued further help. Fortunately, I was led to a chiropractor who was able to identify that I had healed incorrectly and yet had whiplash in my neck and lower back. He worked with me to correct my healing. Pain and discomfort continued and over an eighteen month period I was slowly brought to a place of well-being. Finally I was pain-free once again!

One would imagine that my renewed health would contribute to a real happiness for me. However, I was not happy. I had focused on pain and struggle for too long! I felt little happiness; a victim of a difficult experience.

I read in a book by Sarah Brethnach that the practice of listing five things that I was grateful for - each day before retiring - would afford a change. I felt that it certainly couldn't hurt to try! Some days, I needed to work at finding a list of five things to appreciate. But slowly, I realized that my life held many blessings, if I but see them! I continued.

One month later I not only found this practice to flow much more easily; but also discovered a newfound happiness growing in myself that was not there earlier. Before that time I had always believed that I was powerless over my attitude, but this experience proved me wrong! And I have continued to practice the attitude of gratitude since. I have come to believe that my thoughts are as magnets, drawing to myself what I focus on.

A loving sister of mine reminds me - if I am fretting over a coming event - to send positive thoughts ahead into this event rather than fearful ones. So I've worked at doing that. I find that it makes all the difference in the world!

I am grateful that our former pamphlet spoke of abstaining from negative thinking. The attitude-of-gratitude and positive thinking have become cornerstones of my recovery and life.

Chapter 30

The Value of Validation

I didn't understand why I lost my pain tolerance, but I did. Though sensitive, I did have the ability to walk through any pain that I needed to as a child. But at some point I lost that ability and could not handle pain without a flood of tears.

My Ears, Nose and Throat doctor asked me a question when I went to see him about my ear. "Have you ever considered having the (sizeable) mole removed from your forehead?" he asked. "You'd look nice without it."

I had never considered such a thing before. I had that mole from little on and considered it 'a part of the package' that I came in. My doctor had planted a seed.

One year later, I called that same doctor's office and announced "I'm ready to have my mole removed." We made an appointment. On the day I was scheduled, I came in, lied on my back and was given the Novocain injections that were needed to numb my forehead.

My tears fell immediately and I felt embarrassed. "I'm sorry for the tears, but I have no pain tolerance since my son was born." My doctor asked me, "Oh? How old is your son?" "Five years," I replied. He commented, "That must have been a traumatic experience for you!"

Yes, my son's birth was traumatic for me. But I had not claimed the experience with those words. His birth was recorded as a 'normal vaginal delivery'. Before this day, no one had used those words, or given that validation to my experience.

I went home and found myself mourning the experience that my son's birth was for me. I know that I had felt stretched beyond what I thought I could live through. And after two days of mourning, I felt at peace.

Do you know what? My pain tolerance came back!

Since that day, I do not hesitate to validate or explore words that help clarify whatever another person is sharing with me. That doctor gave me a gift by listening behind my words. I needed the validation of another person to open the door to that healing!

Chapter 31

Heaven Cares

As I shared earlier, I am the third child of six; born to hardworking parents who farmed for a living. I soon had a feeling of worth and belonging for what I could contribute to all that needed to be done on our farm. Since daughters were born before sons, help was needed in the fields, and I enjoyed driving tractors to drag or cultivate the soil, and helped prepare and bale the alfalfa which would then be stored in the barn for feed. I also helped with the harvest of oats and barley, feeling good as I brought loads home to store in our granary, which later would be used to feed cattle and poultry in the winter. Beginning in the seventh grade, I raised chickens which were only one day old until their maturity, when roosters would be slaughtered for meat and hens would be transported to a warmer building for winter, where they could live and lay their eggs.

With my mom, I learned to bake, cook and sew. My siblings and I were each responsible for jobs that needed to be done around the house and praised for our contributions. In the summer, with a large garden, each of us was needed with the harvest, preparation and preserving of vegetables and fruit for our future meals. We knew that we were needed and appreciated.

We were a creative family and encouraged by our mom to develop our creativity. Artistic and musical, we delighted and felt a fierce pride in who we were.

Because I wanted to please my parents and wanted to be a good person, I became very 'tied into' my mother. Dad worked outside, and my preference was to be domestic. So, unless we were working in the garden, field or yard, you could find me in the house. I knew how to get Mom's praise and had a hunger for it. I also knew that my parents' lives were not easy ones; it seemed that they would forego 'extras' for themselves, but always made sure that their children had all the good things that they wanted for us. I felt guilty about this, and tried to make few demands on them.

At Twenty-six, I started to become aware that I desperately needed to be hugged or touched; I realized that I had needs that had not been touched in my idyllic background. I prayed that God would care about my needs and fill this ache that was coming into my awareness.

As my ache seemed to become overpowering, I continued to pray. A few friends arranged for me to date their brothers. I felt flattered, but nothing grew from these arrangements. As shared earlier, I met my husband – to – be at a time when I was feeling empty. Meeting him and dating started to touch this part of me. I began to experience unconditional love.

One year after our wedding, I was led into recovery for my addiction to overeating. It was new and difficult for me to 'own' many of the feelings that I had buried, growing up. In fact, my husband had also buried his feelings as a child. We came into recovery about the same time which was a challenge but also a blessing.

As I worked with my program of recovery, I needed to look at and feel the feelings and needs which I had buried. If I did not, they would continue to fuel my addiction. I came to see unhealthy patterns that I had with my family and life; an overhauling was needed! I **did** want recovery badly enough to begin my fumbling attempts at change. And, my new-found program and friends supported and opened the door for many miracles along the way.

Six years later, my mom had been having health problems when we learned that she had lymphoma. I couldn't imagine my life without her, and mourned in fear as her chemo treatments and stays in the hospital began. It amazed me how peaceful she seemed whenever she was hospitalized; she must have felt secure that her needs would be taken care of in that setting. Yet, death was very fearful for her; she could not talk about the possibility of dying.

At this time, I had my husband and a young son and lived three hours from my parents' home. Although I dreaded losing her, I prayed to God, asking that I might have an opportunity to tell Mom the things I hadn't been able to put into words before, and I also **told** God that I wanted to be with her at the time of her death. I had never prayed this way before; I wondered if my desire would be honored. I was ever so grateful when I felt led to call her one evening. She was very weak and could hardly talk, but I asked if she had the energy to listen. I went on to ask Mom's forgiveness for ways I had caused her pain. **And,** Mom asked for **my** forgiveness for ways that she had hurt me! I also told her I loved her and thanked her for all the gifts she had given to me in life. Now, Mom and I had never had a conversation like this before - or said many of these things. I rejoiced as I felt a great peace inside; and hoped that my mother was feeling the same peace. Still, I knew that she would not live long, and wondered how it could work out for me to be with her when she died.

Ten days later, I received a phone call from my sister-in-law, summoning me to come. My husband was away, but I was able to reach him by phone. And, with several calls, I was able to find a babysitter for our son. I packed quickly, and raced to the city where my family was in the process of gathering.

Not knowing what I'd come to, I did arrive to find my mother incoherent. Still, I touched her and spoke to her. I found consolation in my family members who gathered with me. At least, I was not alone; my father was present, as were my five brothers and sisters and other significant people. We talked and sang and prayed. Later in the evening, several decided to find places to spend the night. A brother and I knew that we wanted to stay in the room with Mom. My brother stayed awake while I napped.

At about 4 a.m., I awoke and told my brother to sleep; I would sit up with Mom. While he rested, Mom went into convulsions; nurses told us that the end was near. We were able to call together our dad, brother and sister who hadn't left town. We prayed together, each touching Mom as we prayed. Just as the sun rose, Mom took her last breath. I felt her warm foot become cool and then warm again; I believed that I felt her spirit as it left her body. It was comforting for each of us to spend time with Mom's body; we stayed for more than an hour before we left.

The month was June, 1987, shortly after my mother's 69th birthday. The weather was very dry, and moisture was badly needed for the crops. As I walked to my car, which was parked about two blocks away, it started to pour rain! My spirit soared! I felt that heaven was celebrating Mom's arrival, and that Mom was celebrating her newfound freedom!

In the wake and funeral that followed, I sincerely felt on a spiritual high. We were surrounded by so much love and kindness. Mom was known by our community for her kindness and generous heart. The funeral home and church were packed! We celebrated our mother's life and death together.

At this time, I had mixed feelings. I knew that I loved and would greatly miss this Mom who gave me all she had to give. Yet, I felt guilty as I realized that my life would feel simpler not having to deal with her fears.

Soon after, I learned that my ear surgery had not been successful. And, in December, I had a miscarriage. I went into depression. During that depression, my relationship with my husband - which had been a refuge for me - became very painful. His childhood feelings, impacted by my depression came roaring out, for my husband had felt emotionally abandoned by his mother who suffered from depression. He screamed his rage at me, not able to see that his feelings were connected to his childhood. After several painful months, I came to know that we needed help. This led to a counselor and many sessions that in time brought us healing, and a new appreciation of the gifts of life and faith.

In my depression and after my losses, I struggled with my own image of God and anger about my trust - and feeling duped by God and life. It was at this time that I sought out a spiritual mentor, who might help me come to deal with my feelings, find healing, and move on from this place. She was a real gift to me at this time. She had experience with grief counseling and knew the principles of my recovery program. She was very intuitive and helped me to learn from my feelings and from my night-time dreams.

At one of our sessions, I was asked who I needed the most. I was not very insightful, which is common during depression; I told her that I didn't know the answer to her question. She suggested that it seemed that I really needed my mother. I agreed. She asked me to go home and write a letter to my mother. She said that I should ask my mother to come and hold me. I wouldn't know *how* she would hold me or *when, but I was to ask Mom to let me know that she was holding me!* I couldn't have imagined making such a request on my own. I knew that I was not hugged or held much growing up. But I trusted this woman and knew that being held by Mom would be a gift at this time. I wrote the letter and waited.

At this time, my husband's work often kept him away overnight. On a cold January morning when he was gone, I awoke at 5:30 a.m. I have an ability to sense the energy of a spirit's presence – and awoke knowing that a spirit was in the bedroom with me! I did not feel alarmed or afraid, but at peace. Gently, I felt my spirit lifted from my body, with my head and feet still 'in' my body; I was draped over a lap! I knew that Mom had come to hold me!!! I spoke with her and attempted to listen, but I heard nothing. So, I chatted on and on, enjoying that I could share with my mom what had all happened to me since her death! I was held for twenty minutes, and then gently laid back down. I felt overjoyed that my mom had come to hold me – that heaven had heard my plea **and** that my spiritual friend had even suggested such a thing! And in June of that year, Mom came to hold me again, this time for an hour! Although I heard no words, I did hear a song in my head. Later, when I listened to this song, I had chills as I heard the words:

"In the morning light you hold me, closer
than the air around me you surround me
always, everywhere I go..."

I listened to that song, "Everywhere I Go" by Amy Grant
many times after that day treasuring the awe I felt during
my experience. What a gift!

I want to share this story, for I've come to know that our
loved ones care greatly about our lives, our needs and our
healing. And, I've come to believe that things are possible
that we might not have ever imagined! It's never too late to
deal with unfinished issues we might have with our deceased
loved one – for **heaven cares**!

Chapter 32

Short Nuggets of Learning and Wisdom

I Have Come to Believe That...

Each of us must learn for ourselves, we cannot learn for another. We cannot even know what's best for another.

෨෬

Nothing happens to us by accident. Each life is tailored to what that soul needs to learn.

෨෬

We are where God needs us to be.

෨෬

To grow we need to release our fears of knowing ourselves, of listening to our hearts and learning who we are.

A tool that helped me in this discernment has been to consider which option or voice in me is most "life-giving". This has helped me find ways I have limited myself, so that I could make new choices!

෨෬

When I was in high school, my father told me that I need to "think for myself and not follow the crowd". I have not forgotten his words. How else could I learn to listen within? Out of fear, I was very indecisive as a young adult. It took many years before I would learn to hear that small voice within, and then even more time to trust it. When I ignored it, I would soon see my error.

My recovery was a gigantic step toward hearing and identifying a 'committee of voices within me and learning which were fear based, limiting, shaming, or healthy, freeing and trustworthy. As I would identify these voices, I could choose which I would follow.

ℰℭ

Our words are also important; they act as a magnet, attracting the very things we focus on. Making a choice and 'stating our intention' opens doors and sets our direction, unless we have made conflicting choices before this which we will need to release.

ℰℭ

I believe that many of us are unaware of the power of choice. Our free will is spiritually honored, absolutely. If I do not choose to ask for help, none will be given. I've learned that asking is important for it truly opens doors for us.

"Ask and it will be given to you; seek and you will find; knock and the door will be opened to you.

For the one who asks always receives; the one who seeks always finds;

The one who knocks will always have the door opened to him."

Matthew 7: 7-8

സ്റ

I believe that all that we leave unresolved in our lives keeps coming back to us until we deal with it. If we do not learn the lessons we need to learn, they will be presented to us in another situation…over and over until we 'get it'. I believe that God and our Angels are infinitely patient with us!

സ്റ

I believe that God does not judge us; we judge ourselves. We live with the consequences of our personal and mankind's actions. Our challenging and difficult times can be times of learning – which **we** chose before we were born. We truly want to learn our soul lessons.

സ്റ

When I try to control anything or anyone, I am not free.

സ്റ

Our free will is honored. God doesn't control. We are allowed the opportunity to experience the outcomes of our choices and grow from them.

☙❧

I have never seen pain as a positive experience. I believe that it is natural to avoid painful situations or to choose what options we feel would cause us less pain. For me, my use of food became my attempt to escape feelings and situations that were uncomfortable for me. My use of certain foods, often carbohydrates, was also an attempt to nurture myself and to lift my feelings. Only over time did I see how self-destructive this was for me!

☙❧

To grow, I must let go of blame and victimhood.

☙❧

Conditional love is saying "I will love you if you do this for me, or if you act in a certain way. God does not love us conditionally. Yet we become conditional as we think "I was being good" or "He was being bad". Judgment keeps us stuck in a place of conditional love.

☙❧

Learning to love, 'no matter what', is to begin to know God's love for us! Did Jesus not come to show us the power of love? Love is powerful. Love conquers. And in love, you and I are free!

80 CR

I believe that we can trust the desires of our hearts, which have stood the test of time. They are important clues to us; parts of our unique selves that lead us to the very things we desire!

80 CR

Waiting is the "stuff" of life. Anything in my life, which was important to me has involved waiting, clarifying, trusting. I would learn in time just how important each desire was for me. When I was impatient, as I 'waited' to come out of depression, a friend once told me "**I** know how to wait. I just distract myself!" Her words held a wisdom that served me in my waiting.

80 CR

You and I may not like what we're going through…but if we consider what we are learning from our experience, we can come to know God's work in our lives.

80 CR

Please use what fits for you and let go of the rest.

Chapter 33

Thoughts Become Form

I had read many times that 'what we think' takes on form in our lives. And, I believe that God wants us to be ourselves fully, to honor our likes and dislikes – in ways that also honor those around us. I've had experiences that have brought this home to me in a real way.

We had lived in our third home for some months, and slowly, the decorations that I wanted to use in it took shape. For some reason, it felt right to take my time and let this be a process. To some, how one decorates their home may seem trivial or unimportant. But for me, I spend much time in our home and take delight in integrity of color and flow within it. My home is my castle!

The original builders used colors and woods that I take delight in, however I felt a need to change some areas.

For instance, in an attempt to carry out a color theme, our bathroom had different shades of blue in it. The bath tiles were an aqua blue, the counter a dark powder blue and white, and the walls yet another shade. In time, I repainted the walls ivory, but considered what I might use to bring together the other two blues, which really did not match!

I decided to keep my eyes open for pictures which would incorporate different blue and in effect, unite them. I remember looking for these pictures for over a year! A belief was growing in me, at that time, that God wanted me to be myself and would honor who I am. I asked for guidance and trusted that I would be led. Besides that, I had others to focus on, with an energetic toddler to fill my days!

I'm sure that it was at least eighteen months later that I found myself enjoying a little time looking in a book and media store. I came upon a section of wall calendars, and automatically considered if any would fit my need. Shortly, I came upon a calendar by an artist whose pictures had colors, themes and style which delighted me…and several incorporated different shades of blue! I bought the calendar and enjoyed choosing which two pieces of art would finish my bathroom decoration! I already had frames and matting; they fit perfectly!

A few other areas of our home presented walls which I wanted to decorate with something new, which would give focus and delight in well used areas. At this time, grapevine wreaths were newly used for decoration. I liked their 'earthiness' and the character of their wood. Each had its own personality; I decided that I wanted to use grapevine wreaths to finish off two walls.

I looked in a nearby floral shop, but cringed when I saw the price tag of any wreaths that I truly liked. It was not in my character to spend a lot of money on decorations! In fact, our budget had its limitations and I had a clear sense of what was too much money! I decided that I would not let go of this hope, but somehow get the materials I needed and make my own! After all, I believe that it is important that I be myself; that 'the Universe' cared about even the things that I find delight in, so I turned over the affair and trusted that I'd be led.

Three days later, my husband had a business trip planned to southern Minnesota and invited me to go along – to an area where one of my former high school friends lived. I had not seen Jane for years, and was glad to join him for the trip. Jane welcomed the opportunity and I spent a lovely afternoon with her in her home while he went about his business. As I came into her home, I gasped as I saw an enormous grapevine wreath(!) decorating a stone fireplace which extended up to their Cathedral ceiling. Of course, with grapevine wreaths on my mind, I shared my adventure with her. My friend responded that she had something new planned to decorate her fireplace and offered to give me this large oval of grapevine! I couldn't believe my ears! It was so large that we could barely get it into the back seat of our car, but we managed and brought it home with us! Now I needed to learn how to work with this wood to dissemble this huge wreath and form two wreaths which would fit our walls. Again, I turned that piece of the project over to heaven.

That evening, I called and visited with my parents. I told my Dad about my new acquisition and interest. "Oh, I know how to soften that vine," he shared, "you need to soak it for several hours in a hot tub of water until it becomes pliable…" Now, I had not only the materials, but also the method!

It wasn't even a week since my idea had come to me and I was able to follow it through! The grapevine was so large that only one-fourth fit into the tub's water at a time! I needed to turn this huge circle regularly to soak it. In about five or six hours, it became flexible. I covered the floor in one room with heavy plastic and soon developed my feel for forming and weaving this wood round and round. Two lovely wreaths were created from one large one.

Chapter 34

Set My Intention

Set my intention.
Unless I do this, I
    am not manifesting my power of choice,
    my power of free will.
I am like a rudderless ship,
    swirling at the mercy of my days
    without direction,
Or like a plow, not set into the earth
    but driving over a field,
    moving no dirt to prepare the soil
    for a new seeding,
    a new harvest.
I need to choose.
What do I intend? Where do I hope to get?
Who do I really want to be?
If I declare my intention,
    my power of choice is active,
    my direction clarified.
I do not know *how* I'll reach my goal,
    but that is not my concern.
I am a spiritual being.
I have help if I ask for it!
And I believe with my whole heart that
    my goal will be reached!

℘℧

There was a time when our extended family planned to spend several days together after Christmas. One of my brothers gifted us with this time, to be spent at a lovely group of lodges in a neighboring state. As I anticipated this, I had it in myself to offer to purchase and cook **all** of the meals which we would have together! I knew well that my feelings could turn on me with such a decision, but decided to try this new tool and 'set my intention'. I stated simply, "I set my intention to let my family know that I love them by doing this." We would be a gathering of fifteen or sixteen.

I over-bought, as I am wont to do, but was aware of only love in my heart during the entire time! What a gift!

Chapter 35

Forever New

"No need to recall the past, no need to
think about what was done before.
See, I am doing something new. Now it springs forth,
Do you not perceive it? In the desert I
make a way, in the wasteland, rivers."
Isaiah 43: 18 – 19

As a child, I looked for God in rituals, and traditions. I felt secure in the repetition of annual faith and prayer events, and our weekly liturgy. I loved the liturgy – so much so that I went to two services each weekend for several years (one with each parent, as little ones were at home). It was not difficult for me to delight in its' rituals and music. And after high school, I entered a convent for five years of schooling and training. But I left five years later, realizing that I desired a husband and children. My heart was leading me; I needed to listen and trust.

So with a very religion – centered life, you can begin to understand why I could not identify with the concept of spiritual bankruptcy. After all, I believed that God existed. However, 'emptying my cup' of all that it held opened the way for me to learn - a new life and freedom I could not have anticipated. My old way of relating to life wasn't working for me. I stepped forward in faith. And I am forever grateful that I was challenged to do that.

I have grown to love the above scripture. I am aware of liking the security of repetition. However, life's reality *is* living with change. Our spiritual path is forever bringing us to new growth and inspiration. I like to call each new day in my life an adventure.

In the Gospel of John (3:8), Jesus says:
"The wind blows wherever it pleases; you hear its' sound,
But you cannot tell where it comes
from or where it is going.
That is how it is with all who are born of the Spirit."

If we have welcomed the Spirit of God into our lives, can you or I predict where we will be called? I do believe that I will be called to more fully be myself! How can I know where another is being led? I could never have predicted that my belief system would change in the ways it has, or that I would ever be led to leave the 12 step program after 29 years, but I was. And I am seeing how I am now being called to claim my strengths, instead of my weaknesses. I am grateful. I have experienced a freedom that I never knew life could hold. And, if I feel limited in any way, I need to consider where *I* am limiting *myself.* I do pray for guidance, and to be led to what is for my highest good. I believe that this is important. Learning this has helped me allow the people around me – including my children – to be wherever they are at in their growth. My gift to them can always be my example, love and prayers.

Part 4

Tools For Living

Chapter 36

My sister taught me a **CLEARING PRAYER** many years ago. She had learned it from author Echo Bodine, who learned it from her teacher, Birdie Torgenson. I share it with their blessing. My sister learned that sensitive people can take on the energy of others and psychically appear as a Christmas tree by the end of the Day! Taking on anothers' energy is not good for us; we each have our own lives and growth to deal with! With my work, I would attend meetings that were charged with someone's emotions and I would be find myself unable to easily let go of the energy I brought home with me. The prayer is simply this:

God, clear my body, clear my mind, clear my spirit and my psyche.

I find the release to be immediate! What a gift!

THE ATTITUDE OF GRATITUDE

As I shared in "Positively", I have learned that choosing to be grateful is essential if you or I find ourselves stuck in negative thinking…It can open the door to happiness.

SEND THEM LIGHT

"Darkness cannot drive out darkness;
only light can do that.
Hate cannot drive out hate; only love can do that.
…I have decided to stick with love. Hate
is too great a burden to bear."

Dr. Martin Luther King Jr.

What a powerful statement by Dr. Martin Luther King Junior! My sister and I have had experiences that echo the wisdom behind his words.

Last summer, my sister had someone come into her fenced back yard and do some damage. Dismayed, she found that a terra cotta statue she loved, which honored Mary, Jesus' mother was smashed. It was evident that this vandalism was done on purpose, for a glass globe stood a few feet away, untouched.

She loved this statue and wrestled with her feelings as she cleaned up its' pieces. Mary's face was yet intact, and she chose to keep that. Back in her home, my sister heard a voice inside her say "Don't send them your anger, send them light."

I have remembered those words since she shared that experience with me. If you or I send anger, we are adding to the darkness. But in sending light, we are asking that the perpetrator be 'enlightened' to see what they are doing and consider the choices they are making. Also, **by choosing to send light, it freed my sister from any darkness she could have carried from that experience**. I do understand that this is not easy to do in some situations. Yet if we hold our anger, we end up suffering from it. We must pray to be led through its' process.

BLESS THEM! This tool is similar to sending light, but I learned it in a different context. One day, I was driving on my way home from a training program that I was attending and got to a point in the avenue where one lane became two. Another driver had been 'on my tail' and seemed impatient. As she zoomed into the second lane and passed me, she gave me 'the finger'! Many times in the past, I would react inwardly and have a difficult time letting go of my feelings. Without thinking, this day I brought up one hand and blessed her!! I surprised myself in doing this, but could only marvel as my feelings immediately were released!

LIFE-GIVING - Be aware of the people and activities in your life that are **life-giving**. We cannot really offer love to others until we learn to love ourselves. It took me time to realize which people or situations were not life-giving for me. As my commitment grew to be loving to myself, I could weed out some of the parts of my life that I found draining. Honor yourself!

LEARN ABOUT YOURSELF! We have many tools available to us to learn about our preferences or what motivates us. As I used several of those tools (e.g. the Myers-Briggs test, the Enneagram). I always found new understanding about my makeup in ways that were very freeing!

WHAT DO YOU NEED? As a new parent, it took me time to realize how healthy it was for me to take time out from my daily tasks. At first, my husband was able to free me to do this. But later, when he was no longer available, I had learned the value of that time well enough to feel positive about taking them to day-care. Our sons are already grown, and I still take time out of the house for a couple of hours, several days each week to read, journal and pray. That has been good for me.

SET YOUR INTENTION. As I get caught up in things, I often forget how important it is to stop and choose what my intent is before diving into a project. But I've been amazed at what happens when I remember to stop, choose what I hope to experience or who I hope to be before I continue.

PUT IT IN GOD'S HANDS. This last November, as I considered what all I wanted to accomplish in the days ahead, I reflected on other years, when I would push myself through card-writing, or gift-wrapping in preparation for the Christmas season, not enjoying what I was doing at all. Did I need to let go of some of these activities? What came to me is the reminder to list all of the tasks I wished to accomplish, and put them in God's hands! (I need a lot of reminders as I grow.) In fact, I decided to ask that I would not only accomplish all that I wanted to do, but also to enjoy doing it!! I was amazed at how 'sane' and enjoyable the month ahead turned out to be!

FOLLOW YOUR HEART. I have come to believe that the desires of my heart are God's way of leading me. Early on, I feared asking to do God's will, because I was afraid that God would ask me to be a missionary in Timbuktu; and I *didn't want* to be a missionary and go there! It was *so* freeing to realize that God's will for me was linked with the very things I desired for myself! My heart's desires did not come to me quickly; I learned that waiting is a big part of trusting. It added to my joy as a desire came to fruition!

QUIET TIME – Our souls need times of quiet.

When I was younger, I was not at peace with myself, and times of quiet would drive me crazy! We live in a world where we are bombarded with music, televisions playing, texting or phone calls and are uncomfortable with a lack of sound and stimulation. We also develop addictions and compulsions in our attempt to escape our inner feelings.

My process of moving toward a desire for silence was gradual. I had much to deal with. But I did need to realize that my discomfort with quiet time told me that many voices were screaming out – inside of me – asking for my attention. I was very needy as a young adult. I didn't like that, but now realize how important it was for me to listen, own those needs and work with spiritual help on dealing with them. They were brought to the foreground of my awareness in a timely manner; I know that I was led through that process. In time, I've come to a place where silence is essential for me to find balance in my day, find peace in my soul, and hear 'that small, still voice within'.

GUIDANCE – We can each work with our 'guides'; it just takes practice! We each have at least one guide, and can trust that we will be led toward our highest good.

To hear my guidance, I was coached to ask my question, and then put my mind in neutral to listen for an answer. In time, I came to find how often the first thing I had 'pop' into my mind was 'right on' for me. And I ask for guidance with small as well as large needs and desires.

On Valentine's Day, one year, I decided to purchase a heart-shaped helium balloon for each person that would come to a meeting that I was attending. The number of participants varied – anywhere from three to ten people would come. I decided to ask for guidance on how many I would need to buy. The number six popped into my mind, so I purchased six balloons and went on my way. Sure enough, five members came that day – and I had one balloon for myself to enjoy!

My guide has been very helpful in helping me remember important things also. I did ask 'her' to help me with this for my memory doesn't always serve me well! We do need to ask. Our power of choice and free will are honored by spirit.

One thing that I've really appreciated has been times that I've asked for guidance as to where I could find some item I needed to purchase…perhaps my time was limited, or I just didn't want to go to several stores to search it out. After asking, I'd listen, and then trust the answer I was given. Inevitably, I'd drive to that very store and find exactly what I was looking for. In fact, already twice, I was told by the store's clerks that they did not have what I was looking for. I persisted in looking after the clerks left me, (after all, I had been *led* there…) and sure enough, I found the very item I had come looking for in their store!!!

Such experiences with the small stuff of life have helped me to know that I can ask for guidance in larger things and trust that my answer will come, though not always immediately. And when it comes, whatever it is, the answer will be for my highest good.

I often speak to my Guide or Guardian Angel and at times call on the Holy Spirit, God or a Saint. I believe that it's more important to learn to ask and less important who we call on!

Part 5

Reflections

Chapter 37

In His Image

Sparks of life
bequeath in beauty,
all is given
that we need.
If we honor
guidance given
we'll know love,
our spirits freed.

Tender mercy
freely given
flows in love
for you, for me.
We're created
in this image –
how could fear
or malice be?
Gentle Father,
loving Mother,
can a name
reflect your might?
We're created
in your image
wondrous beings
from your light.

How you want,
O loving God for
us to live and
grow in you.
With free will we
want our own way,
just as children
often do.

Chapter 38

Noble In Truth

Do you not know that you have
noble blood
flowing through your veins?
Son or daughter of God,
brother or sister of a king,
princes and princesses,
how can we not hold our heads high!
You and I serve
as an Ambassador of our heritage,
our blood line,
in each encounter that we have.
How could we not
carry ourselves uprightly
and be aware of
the nobility that we carry?

Chapter 39

Living Film

Like the film in a camera
we are exposed to life.
Our impressions are formed against
the background of all that we know
as an infant, child and youth.
Memories are like pictures
which capture our home life
and family,
and those significant to us.

I've heard it said that memories
are based on feelings.
Would it not follow that without feelings,
we would have no memories?
I know of people with few memories,
especially of their childhoods.
I feel sad for them,
for buried memories
are connected with buried feelings.

Feelings and memories are
always part
of our inner storehouse,
for all is captured within us
in every cell.

Isn't it interesting that our films
are called 'negatives' and that
which is dark on them
in actuality turns out light
when they are developed?
Also, that which seems
light on negatives
is really dark when developed?
Without contrasts, negatives would hold
no impression at all!
Both light and dark are parts of a whole...
they help us to see more clearly

It seems to me that
when impressions are held,
such as hurt, anger or jealousy,
those impressions color our lense
and affect our memories.
New pictures are taken
through their hue.
Their tint stays with us
until we desire for our lenses to be cleaned
with help from the Master
and our forgiveness.
We must desire and ask for this help
for our free wills are honored!

Gently - and sometimes in a way
that seems to take forever,
we can forgive and be cleaned
to take in a truer, clearer light.

In fact, new light can be brought
into our impressions already formed
and change our perspective
in a memory we've held!

I'm learning that I can
look into a memory that to me seems
quite dark - negative...
And I can send a beam of light
(a new understanding)
into its picture
which affects my entire impression!

The film of my life is very
personal, indeed,
but it is not static!
(It is as if we are using 'living film'!)
I can work with my feelings and the Master
on the impressions I hold!
I have the ability to choose
more than I've ever known!

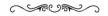

Chapter 40

To Honor

Recycling is a practice that honors the earth...

By recycling, man takes responsibility for what he has created and used.
After all, are we not stewards?

I believe that we honor the earth, God's creatures and each other as we honor ourselves; do they not go together?

I've also started to wonder if we might not go through a series of belief systems as we grow and develop. We always project out from ourselves what we believe in our hearts.
Does not a child think and perceive as a child?
Would we not then try to fit God, others and ourselves into the perception that we carry?
At each stage, we attempt to make sense of life from where we are at.
Would we not also project what we believe onto God?

I have learned that it is important to honor each person in their belief system just as it is important to honor each in how they cope. We each cope with the skills that we have developed up to that point in our life.

Can we ask someone to be more than they are?

No; we must each be ourselves.

Honor yourself!

I know I am limited and cannot control the choices people around me make.

I choose to be as responsible as I can for the things I use.

Most fast food restaurants use high grades of plastic but have no recycling receptacle available. I choose to recycle the items I use, so I take them home, wash them and recycle them in the wonderful bin our city provides. I have requested that places I frequent consider adding a receptacle for recyclable plastics and paper. I am aware of one such place searching out what they might put in. Occasionally I offer to recycle the plastics for other customers, bringing to their awareness that this is important.

Styrofoam items are especially problematic because most recycling programs do not deal with them. However, some communities do!

I happen to have a friend in one such community. I save my Styrofoam and sent it to her 1 to 2 times a year. Her community has a plant which reforms it into underlayment for highways!

Check it out for yourself!

These items do not decompose and sometimes, if they do, it takes centuries!

My eldest son and I used to go, bag in hand, on recycling walks when he was little. He recycles now as an adult, in his own home.

I choose to honor the earth!

Chapter 41

Finishing Unfinished Business - A Wren for a Bird House

My father is remembered by his children and grandchildren for many things. He was playful with his grandchildren and was a great story-teller. Our sons loved when he came to our home and put them to bed with some of his stories. I recorded several of his stories and songs and had a music CD created professionally for each of his grandchildren, so that they could enjoy hearing Grandpa whenever they wished to!

Dad had extensive experience and knowledge of trees, birds and wine-making, among other things. He also had a domestic side which gave him many skills in the kitchen and home. When Mom died after a bout with cancer, we all missed her, of course and it eased our minds that Dad had the ability to cook and do the laundry for himself. He did not mend clothing, however. I chuckled to learn that he found a 'Tear Mender' glue and would patch his overalls using that! He was very creative!

One project that Mom had started and was unable to finish was decorating a pair of pillow cases for each grandchild. Knowing this, Dad picked up where Mom had left off and stitched decorations onto enough pillow cases to make sure that each grandchild had one set!

Years later, my sister took up the creative project of weaving round throw rugs on a wagon wheel. Many of her siblings were gifted with one of these rugs, with colors carefully chosen to match their homes. For the last year-and-one-half of her life, my sister battled with two cancers. She underwent chemotherapy, which was a challenging time for her. She chronicled and illustrated a book about that journey; her dream was to have it published. Dad supported that project and, with her siblings, made sure that her dream was fulfilled. My sister lost her battle with health issues and died. Dad tackled and finished the last of her circular rugs, which had been unfinished in her living space.

One time, Dad made a wren house for our son, Aaron's birthday. He told his grandson all about house wrens, which are rather small birds, and Aaron hung his birdhouse from a branch on a tree in front of our home. Dad, who lived 143 miles from us, asked Aaron several times that summer if his wren house had an occupant. No feathered friends came that first year. And each year after that, Dad would ask Aaron if his house yet had an occupant. Each time, Aaron had to tell his Grandpa that no bird had moved in! Grandpa couldn't figure out why a wren had not made itself at home in 'their' house. He wondered if there might be another wren in our neighborhood, and if wrens were territorial! By now, the wren house was well weathered, which birds seem to prefer. But a wren still hadn't moved in.

Some years later, Dad was diagnosed with stomach cancer and died after six months. We all loved and missed our Dad. But we did not want him to suffer any longer, which helped us to let go. Our Mom, Sister and Dad each had left a legacy for us to treasure and remember them with!

The spring after Dad's death, I worked in our yard one day and heard a clear and melodic song nearby; it was a song I had not heard before. My heart leapt as I saw a tiny wren fly into the house that Grandpa had built and Aaron had cherished. That house had hung in our yard already for eleven years without an occupant…I felt as if my Dad had sent us this beautiful little wren! And our wren returns to its home each spring! What a delight! Alas, now it's nine years later and Grandpa's bird house had become unfixable after several repairs in its lifetime. Aaron carefully measured its dimensions and built another, hoping that our wren would return and move in. And indeed, it has. I feel gratitude each spring when our little friend returns!

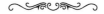

Chapter 42

Words From My Guide

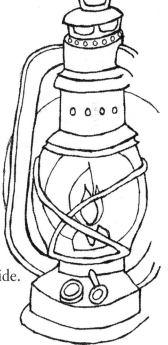

I asked my Guide to speak to me.
 This is what I heard:

You ask for words from me,
 your spirit guide.
Live in the Light, for it is
 in the Light that you grow.
The Light is your guide from inside.
Be at peace. You are led.
Enjoy the moment.
Be satisfied with
 what you are about right now.
That is where God can be found.

Chapter 43

I Am Decidedly a Deciduous Tree

I am decidedly a deciduous tree.
Bedecked with beautiful blossoms in my springtime,
each poses the promise of potential.
Who would not thrive in this season of hope!
Yet there comes a time when growth pushes me on.

The splendor of summer supports new shoots and leaves
reliant on rain, resources, reality,

stilted or supported by surrounding conditions.
(Yet, I can make choices!)
I bask in the warmth and productivity of this season.
A time of fulfillment...

The fullness of fruit: a feast for the soul...
Fall: a golden season of harvest.
But with the harvest comes a need to let go
of warmth and growth. (I feel melancholic.)
Leaves fade and fall.
A season of letting go, of release.

The season of snow and surrender follows.
Life pulls in to protect its essence.
Winter waits its' while.
Dare I dream that the embrace of warmth
And fullness of growth may come again?

In time, the promise of resurrection gives hope.
I continue on, almost unaware of my growth.

Chapter 44

Words Given

Often, I am given words;
they seem to come to me, through me.
Sometimes I do not even fully know their meaning.
I will look them up in the dictionary
and always marvel,
for they are exactly what I want to say.

Chapter 45

Be Yourself!
(A Lesson I've Learned from My Garden)

The leek, it leaked.
Its life spilled forth
from seed that cracked and split;
pungent plant alit.

The beet, it beat
the other plants
with color, deep crimson hue;
makes delightful pickles, too!

The pea, it didn't
but kept its juice
to flavor fruit so fine
on which a king may dine.

The cantaloupe,
it can't elope
but must stay in its place
until our table it grace.

The bean can 'bean'
the best of them
prolific pod or seed
on which a crowd may feed!

Kathleen E. Brummer

The cauliflower, it
does not shower
the garden with colors bright
but hides its color, white.

The squash, it doesn't
lord it over
plants or bugs or you,
but gently drinks its dew.

Brussels sprouted,
on thick stem grew
round green balls to eat;
for some, they are a treat!

Each plant has
been itself and grown
in beauty and service, too;
a model for me and you!

I count myself blessed
to plant these seeds
and have my garden grow;
gift of beauty and food to sow.

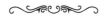

As I Close

I feel that my life has been blessed in so many ways. And for that, I am grateful!

Spirituality has always been my 'bread and butter'. As I reflect on my life, I can see the progression of my growth, and the ways that I was led to learn. Growth does not come gracefully for us, I believe. We tend to grow as the seasons change…back, and forth…back, and forth…back, and forth. I am reminded to be gentle with myself and learn patience along the way.

As I review my writing, I've noticed how many of my 'issues' are repeated several times in my story. What came to me is that before I came into recovery, I *did* go over and over these things. They did not change and I did not know how to resolve them. My miracles began when I gave my heart and soul to my program of recovery, opening the door for me to release the past and live in each day. If you are burdened by any part of your past, I wish the same miracles for you!

We really do need each other. I was reminded of this as a friend shared her struggles with me, and I could speak to what she needed to hear. AND, just weeks later, I shared my struggles with her…and she told me the very same words I had told her – I needed to hear them! When I am in a situation, it takes time to be graced with insight, and many times that insight has come through a friend or family member.

An avid reader, I have often felt my heart leap as the words I read speak to my questions and wondering.

Another tool which has been valuable for me is writing. Sometimes I do not realize that I feel a certain way until it plops down on paper. Or, the very thing I need to hear comes through in my writing.

I must remind myself to release my 'image' of myself and others and allow us to grow! We are each works in progress.

I thank all the experiences and people who have taught me, even when I haven't liked what I was learning!

I thank my guides for their patience and encouragement! God Bless us each in our journey!

Remember to take what you like, and leave the rest.

Printed in the United States
By Bookmasters